What Is Marketing?

Alvin J. Silk
Content Adviser

Harvard Business School Press
Boston, Massachusetts

Copyright 2006 Harvard Business School Publishing Corporation
All rights reserved
Printed in the United States of America
11 10 09 07 06   5 4 3 2

Library of Congress Cataloging-in-Publication Data
What is marketing?
     p.   cm. — (What is ? series)
   ISBN-13: 978-1-4221-0460-6
   1. Marketing. I. Harvard Business School Press.
   HF5415.W483 2006
   658.8—dc22

                                                                2006021351

What Is
Marketing?

Contents

Contents

Part III
Implementing Marketing Strategies

Introduction

IN *THE PRACTICE OF MANAGEMENT,* PETER F. DRUCKER wrote, "There is only one valid definition of business purpose: to create a customer . . . [Therefore], any business enterprise has two—and only these two—basic functions: marketing and innovation. They are the entrepreneurial functions. Marketing is the distinguishing, the unique function of the business."[1] This book explores what marketing is and how an enterprise can differentiate itself from others in attracting and retaining customers.

In general terms, *marketing* refers to what an organization must do to create and exchange value with customers. In this sense, marketing has a major role to play in setting a firm's strategic direction. Successful marketing requires both a deep knowledge of customers, competitors, and collaborators and great skill in deploying an organization's capabilities so as to serve customers profitably.

Marketing, thus defined, is a broad general management responsibility, not just a function delegated to specialists. Anyone with career interests that lead to the setting and the execution of the strategy of an organization, regardless of its type or size, will require marketing skills and insight. Therefore, this book provides the foundation on which to begin developing those skills and insights applicable in a wide variety of situations: in the old economy as well as in the new; in both service and manufacturing sectors; and in business-to-consumer and business-to-business settings, to name a few.

Structure of the Book

The book is organized according to the design of the first-year marketing course in the two-year MBA program at the Harvard Business School (HBS). Each chapter of the book is based on materials written by HBS faculty and used by MBA students in preparation for classroom participation. The book consists of three parts: the analysis of marketing opportunities, the formulation of marketing strategy, and the execution of that strategy.

Part I, "Analyzing Marketing Opportunities," focuses on gaining insights into customers' needs and behaviors, which should guide a company's analysis of its marketing opportunities and form the basis of any viable marketing strategy.

- Chapter 1, "Marketing Strategy," presents a set of conceptual frameworks that organize marketing thought and provides a structure for understanding and analyzing marketing problems and decisions. Figure 1-1, "Schematic of Marketing Process," offers a useful set of topical headings (e.g., the five Cs and the four Ps) that serve to outline and organize the remaining chapters. The appendix to chapter 1, "Basic Marketing Mathematics," defines key terms and basic calculations useful in real-life marketing analysis and decision making.

- Chapter 2, "Understanding Consumer Behavior," introduces concepts that help organizations to understand the decision-making and consumption behavior of both individual consumers and business customers. It argues that the competitive advantage one firm may gain over another frequently arises from its superior understanding of its customers *and* a superior process for thinking about and acting on this information.

Chapter 2 is the longest and arguably the most critical chapter in the book because, if a company does not understand its customers relative to its market opportunities, then the odds of its marketing strategy's success—no matter how otherwise clever, unique, or well executed—are greatly diminished.

Part II, "Developing Marketing Strategies," covers the main components of marketing strategy, often referred to as the "four *P*s"—product (positioning and design), placement (distribution), promotion (communication), and pricing—and touches on branding and brand management as a theme throughout the five chapters.

- Chapter 3, "Market Segmentation, Target Market Selection, and Positioning," constitutes the requisite steps in designing a successful marketing strategy. These steps guide the firm in focusing its efforts on the right customers and in identifying how the different elements in the marketing mix will influence the decisions and behavior of those customers. Formulation of a positioning strategy requires specification of both the target market and the bases upon which a product or service offering can be differentiated from competition.

- Chapter 4, "Product Policy," explores the key issues related to the firm's market offering—be that a product, a service, or a bundle of the two—and covers such topics as new product and service design and development, product line scope, branding, and the repositioning of an existing business. Brands are recognized to be intangible assets that have market value, and the appendix to chapter 4, "Brand Valuation," discusses one approach to assessing brand equity.

- Chapter 5, "Going to Market," covers the functions that must be performed when a firm goes to market with its goods and services (from demand generation and fulfillment to after-sale service) and the distribution channels where those functions are performed, whether the channel is direct to customers or indirect, through retailers and whole-salers, or some combination of both. Key issues relate to the design and management of distribution networks, especially in an era of continuing developments in information and communications technology and the evolution of the Internet.

- Chapter 6, "Marketing Communications and Promotions," covers the need for building demand for a firm's market offerings through media advertising, public relations, and a wide variety of customer and trade promotions.

- Chapter 7, "Optimal Pricing," covers price's role in the mar-keting mix—namely, to tap into the value created so as to generate revenues sufficient to fund the firm's current and future value-creation activities plus yield a profit.

Part III, "Implementing Marketing Strategies," looks at the exe-cution of marketing strategy, specifically at managing and deliver-ing marketing programs through salespeople and building and managing profitable customer relationships.

- Chapter 8, "Personal Selling and Sales Management," explains how the success of any marketing strategy depends on exe-cution and explores both the role of the salesperson and the management of the selling effort.

- Chapter 9, "Managing Customers," deals with customer relationship management and addresses such topics as customer acquisition and retention, customer lifetime value, customer selection and dismissal, and consumer privacy.

How to Use This Book

Management education is similar to training for other professions in that emphasis is placed on the identification and analysis of problems and opportunities in a variety of contexts, the recommendation of the best course of action to address a problem or exploit an opportunity, and the effective and efficient implementation of decisions.

These chapters were developed for use at the Harvard Business School, where each session of a course typically consists of a discussion, by members of the class, of a case describing a real-life business situation that features the dilemma of a real person with a real job and a real problem to solve. Each chapter provides general but durable background knowledge that will help students—current or prospective managers—to grapple with the marketing problem that they confront. This book is intended to support, rather than substitute, for other critical aspects of a student's educational experience, within and outside the classroom. The book lends itself to use in combination with other materials relating to contemporary business and economic developments, cases, articles, guest lecturers, simulations, and fieldwork. Hence, this book should be useful in a wide variety of educational settings and especially to instructors seeking to tailor their course content to the needs of a particular audience.

At the ends of chapters, there are lists of additional readings and resources as well as chapter notes for further study. These readings and resources provide both current and classic thinking on the chapter's topics. However you choose to master the fundamentals of marketing, we hope that you find this volume of lasting use, and we wish you the best in your endeavors.

—Alvin J. Silk

Lincoln Filene Professor of Business Administration, Emeritus
Harvard Business School
Boston, Massachusetts

Notes

1. Peter F. Drucker, *The Practice of Management* (New York: Harper-Collins Publishers, 1954).

Part I

Analyzing Marketing Opportunities

Marketing Strategy

THE CENTRAL ROLE OF MARKETING IN THE ENTER-prise stems from the fact that **marketing** is the process via which a firm creates value for its chosen customers. Value is created by meeting customer needs. Thus, a firm must define itself not by the product it sells, but by the customer benefit provided.[1]

Having created the value for its customers, the firm is then entitled to capture a portion of that value through pricing. To remain a viable concern, the firm must sustain this process of creating and capturing value over time. Within this framework, the plan by which value is created on a sustained basis is the firm's **marketing strategy**. Marketing strategy involves two major activities: (1) selecting a target market and determining the desired positioning of the product in target customers' minds and (2) specifying the plan for the marketing activities to achieve the desired positioning. In these activities, **positioning** is the unique selling proposition for the product. Figure 1-1 presents a schematic describing a general process of marketing strategy development.

This chapter was written by Robert J. Dolan and originally published as "Note on Marketing Strategy," Class Note 9-598-061 (Boston: Harvard Business School Publishing, 1997). It was lightly edited for consistency.

FIGURE 1-1

Schematic of marketing process

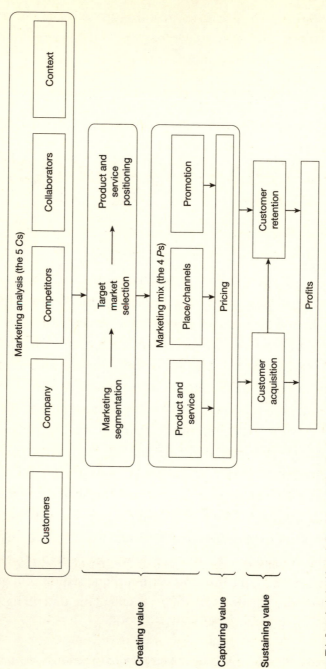

Source: This figure is derived from similar representations developed over the years by Harvard Business School marketing faculty and other academics.

As shown, five major areas of analysis underlie marketing decision making. The discussion here begins with analysis of the five *C*s—customers, company, competitors, collaborators, and context. Questions to consider include:

1. Customer needs: What needs does the firm seek to satisfy?

2. Company skills: What special competence does the firm possess to meet those needs?

3. Competition: Who competes with the firm in meeting those needs?

4. Collaborators: Whom should the firm enlist to help it and how can the firm motivate them?

5. Context: Which cultural, technological, and legal factors limit the possibilities?

This leads first to specification of a target market and desired positioning and then to the marketing mix. This results in customer acquisition and retention strategies driving the firm's profitability.

This introductory chapter develops this framework. It first sets out the major decisions to make and then elaborates on the five *C*s analysis required to support effective decision making, but it does not present the actual analytical techniques. However, the additional readings and resources listed at the end of the chapter contain in-depth coverage of the issues.[2]

Target Market Selection and Product Positioning

Marketing strategy development begins with the customer.[3] A prerequisite to the development of the rest of the marketing strategy is specification of the target markets the company will attempt to serve. Marketers have generally been moving from serving large mass markets to specification of smaller segments with customized marketing programs. Indeed, a popular phrase today is "markets of one," suggesting that marketing campaigns can and should be customized to individuals. In the days of "you can have any color you want as long as it's black," production capabilities and limited information on consumers' varying wants acted as constraints on the development of programs customized to individual consumers. Now new technologies enable firms to practice customized marketing on an economical basis in many situations.[4]

The two key questions are:

1. Which potential buyers should the firm attempt to serve? To answer this, the firm must first determine the most appropriate way to describe and differentiate customers. This is the process of **segmentation**.

2. How much customization should the firm offer in its programs—that is, at which point on the continuum from

    Mass Market – Market Segments – Market Niches – Individuals

    will the firm construct plans?

Markets can be segmented in a variety of ways.[5] Among the most widely used bases are:

- Demographic (e.g., age, income, gender, occupation)

- Geographic (e.g., nation, region of country, urban vs. rural)

- Lifestyle (e.g., hedonistic vs. value oriented)

These three types of bases—demographic, geographic, and lifestyle—are general descriptors of consumers. Often, a useful segmentation of the market is derived by using segmentation bases that describe a customer's behavior or relationship to a product. See table 1-1 for an example.

Consider a personal computer manufacturer segmenting the market on the basis of user status. One might choose to target first-time home-use computer buyers; another may target mainly those who already own but wish to trade up. The firms' explicit choice of

TABLE 1-1

Example of segmentation based on customer behavior

User status	Nonuser vs. user
Usage rate	Light, medium, heavy user
Benefits sought	Performance oriented vs. price oriented
Loyalty status	None, moderate, strong, totally loyal
Attitude toward product	Unsatisfied, satisfied, delighted

target markets has obvious, important implications for the features to be included in their computers and for their communications efforts. Segmentation schemes yielding these clear implications for marketing are most useful. There is little point in using a segmentation basis to define groups to be marketed to in the same way.

The process of selecting the segments to serve is critical because ultimately the customer has the right to dictate the rules via which the marketing game will be played (i.e., a customer uses the purchase criteria that customer decides to use, and these in effect are the "rules of the game"). Thus, the firm's selecting a target market is tantamount to choosing the rules of the game, and consequently target market selection should consider:

- The firm's comparative strengths and weaknesses vis-à-vis competition given the target market's purchase criteria

- The firm's corporate goals and the fit of the segment with these goals

- The resources necessary to market successfully to the target segment

- The need for/availability of appropriate collaborators to market successfully

- The likely financial returns from the segment

FIGURE 1-2

Fill-in-the-blank positioning statement

_____	is	_____
Our product/brand		(single most important claim)
		_____
among all		(competitive frame)
		_____
because		(single most important support)

As part of the segmentation and target market selection process, the firm has to play out scenarios. That is, it must consider the question, if we pursue this segment, how would we approach it, and how would we want potential buyers to see us? The answer should be formalized in a positioning statement specifying the position the firm wishes to occupy in the target customers' minds.[6] The precise form of a positioning statement can vary, but a useful form is shown in figure 1-2.

In some cases, the positioning cannot be sufficiently well captured via a focus on the single most important claim (e.g., a computer manufacturer may want to be seen as both easy to use and fast, so the positioning statement form can be adjusted). But an explicit statement of the positioning idea is critical.

The absolute importance of target market selection and positioning is well conveyed in a best-selling marketing textbook: "The advantage of solving the *positioning problem* is that it enables the company to solve the *marketing mix problem*. The marketing mix—product, price, place, and promotion—is essentially the working out of the tactical details of the positioning strategy."[7]

The Marketing Mix

Neil Borden of Harvard Business School used the term **marketing mix** to describe the set of activities comprising a firm's marketing program.[8] He noted how firms blend mix elements into a program and how even firms competing in a given product category can have dramatically different mixes at work. He specified twelve mix elements:

1. Merchandising/product planning

2. Pricing

3. Branding

4. Channels of distribution

5. Personal selling

6. Advertising

7. Promotions

8. Packaging

9. Display

10. Servicing

11. Physical handling

12. Fact finding and analysis/market research

Over time, an aggregation and regrouping of these elements has become popular. As shown in figure 1-1, the four *P*s of product, price, promotion, and place are often used to set out the marketing mix in an easy-to-recall way. The discussion will now turn to the major issues in setting the four *P*s in the following sequence:

1. Product

2. Place (channels of distribution)

3. Promotion (communications strategy)

4. Pricing

Product

Product Definition

Product decisions start with an understanding of what a **product** is—namely, the product offering is not the thing itself, but rather the total package of benefits obtained by the customer. This idea has had a number of names (e.g., the *total product concept, the augmented product*, or *the integrated product*). For marketing strategy development purposes, the product has to be considered from the point of view of value delivered to the customer. Value can be delivered simultaneously by a number of vehicles, for example:

- The physical product itself

- Brand name

- Company reputation

- Presale education provided by salespeople

- Postsale technical support

- Repair service

- Financing plans

- Convenient availability

- Word-of-mouth references from earlier adopters of the product

- Reputation of the outlet where the product was purchased

For example, a shirt from the Lands' End catalog is not just a shirt but one shipped within twenty-four hours of order and unconditionally guaranteed.[9] This broad conception of a product is key to seeing possible points of differentiation from competitors.

Product Line Planning Decisions

A taxonomy of product line planning decisions is best developed by considering examples of some product planning decisions firms face:

- Product line breadth: A desktop computer manufacturer considers also selling laptops; a maker of men's golf attire considers adding a women's line; an automobile manufacturer considers a minivan or sport-utility vehicle. Product line breadth decisions are how many different lines the company will offer. A guiding principle in answering breadth questions is the company's position on desired consistency or similarity between the lines it offers. Some firms say, for example, "We market only products that draw on our skills in small-motor technology," while others are more broad, "We sell products that draw on our superior consumer products marketing skills."

- Product line length: A beer producer in the mass part of the market is considering whether it should develop an entry in the premium segment; the high-end computer manufacturer considering the product line breadth issue just discussed also has to decide whether it wants to compete in the emerging "under $999" market sector. These are product line length decisions—that is, how many items there will be in a line providing coverage of different price points.

- Product line depth: The men's golf attire manufacturer considers whether to offer its $110 crew neck sweater in five colors or just three. Thus, this decision addresses product line depth that is, how many types of a given product there will be.

These are the three major types of product line planning decisions. Important considerations in making these decisions are:

- Does the product satisfy target customer wants in a way that is profitable for the firm?

- Does it offer opportunity for differentiation from competitors when the "product" is appropriately viewed as the total set of benefits delivered to consumers?

- What is the impact of this product on the rest of the line? Will it be a complement to other products, enhancing their value to the customer (e.g., a color-coordinated sweater enhancing the value of the matching golf shirt), or will it be a substitute, possibly cannibalizing sales (e.g., an entry in the low end of the personal computer market taking sales from the same manufacturer's high-end, higher-margin items)?

- What is the impact of the items on the brand and company's reputation? The brand's equity is often a key asset, and the product may enhance it or may detract from it. A key issue is whether there would be damage to the brand. For example, did Lipton Soup detract from the company's equity as a tea supplier, did Sears Financial Network hurt Sears' retail operations?[10]

Individual Item Decisions

As reflected in the previous discussion, decisions on individual items must be considered within the context of the firm's full product line due to item interrelationships. At the individual item level, decisions to be made are whether to undertake efforts to:

- Delete an item from the line

- Reposition an existing product within the line

- Improve the performance of an existing product to strengthen its positioning

- Introduce a new product within an existing line

- Introduce a product to establish a new line

The New Product Development Process

Generally, a proactive approach to new product development follows some form of a sequential process—for example, a five-step process of:

1. Opportunity identification

2. Design

3. Testing

4. Product introduction

5. Life cycle management[11]

In the opportunity identification stage, the firm identifies a customer problem that it can solve. In addition, it identifies the concept for a product to ensure both a product-market fit (the product fits the needs of the customer) and a product-company fit (it fits with the manufacturing and operational skills of the firm).

The next two stages of design and testing are linked in an iterative process. For example, the firm might first embody the product idea in a concept statement, which is tested via presentation to potential customers. Given a favorable reaction, the concept could then be developed into a mock-up to permit more effective communication of what the product would look like when actually marketed. An unfavorable reaction from consumers in any testing results in an iteration back to the design stage.

Testing with consumers can be done via a number of procedures—for example, surveys, taste tests, simulated test markets (in which mock stores are set up and consumers recruited to shop in the mock store environment), and actual test markets for consumer goods and beta tests for industrial goods.[12] Testing is appropriate not only for the product itself but also for the supporting elements of the marketing mix, such as the communications strategy and price.

After the firm has settled on the product and a supporting plan, it reaches product introduction. Decisions at this stage involve the geographic markets to which the product will be introduced and whether markets will be approached at the same time or sequentially over time (e.g., a regional rollout).

After introduction, a process of product life cycle management begins. First, the firm should continually be learning more about consumers from their reactions to the introduced product. This added learning may suggest product repositioning or marketing mix changes. Second, the marketing environment is always changing. For example, customer wants are not static; market segment sizes change; competitive offerings change; technology impacts the firm's capabilities and costs. Thus, managing the product line is a dynamic process over time.

Place: Marketing Channels

The **marketing channel** is the set of mechanisms or the network via which a firm goes to market—that is, is in touch with its customer for a variety of tasks ranging from demand generation to physical delivery of the goods. The customer's requirements for effective support determine the functions that the members of the channel must collectively provide. V. Kasturi Rangan of Harvard Business School has identified eight generic channel functions that serve as a starting place for assessing needs in a particular context:

1. Product information

2. Product customization

3. Product quality assurance

4. Lot size (e.g., the ability to buy in small quantities)

5. Product assortment (refers to breadth, length, and width of product lines)

6. Availability

7. After-sale service

8. Logistics[13]

An important point with respect to channel design is that while there are options about whether a particular institution (e.g., a distributor) is included in the channel or not, the setting implicates specific tasks that must be accomplished by someone in the channel. One can eliminate a layer in the chain but not the tasks that layer performed. The popular phrase "we've cut out the middleman and passed the savings on to you" seems to indicate that the middleman represents all costs but no value added. The functions done by the middleman now have to be done by someone else. Thus, the recommended approach is to develop customer-driven systems assessing the channel structure and management mechanisms that will best perform the needed functions.[14]

The two major decisions in channels are:

1. Channel design, which involves both a length and breadth issue

2. Channel management—that is, what policies and procedures will be used to have the necessary functions performed by the various parties

Channel Design

With an understanding of customer requirements in place, a primary question in channel design is whether distribution will be direct, indirect, or both (i.e., some customers served one way and others another). In **direct distribution**, there is no independent party between the firm and its customers—for example, the "blue suits" of the firm's sales force visit the customer premises and sell computer mainframes. Through 1980, this was the only way IBM sold its products. In **indirect distribution**, there is a third party. This party may operate under contract to the firm (e.g., as in a franchise system), or it may act independently (e.g., as in a situation where a retailer pays for and takes title to the firm's goods and then is free to sell them at whatever price and in whatever fashion it desires).

Through the 1960s, the conventional wisdom was that a firm should go to market either direct or indirect, but not both, because of the channel conflict that would result. The bias was toward going direct as soon as sales volume justified it, because direct distribution provided more control and direct contact with customers.

By the early 1980s, more firms began simultaneously serving different target markets, each requiring different channel functions (e.g., one segment needed intense presale education; another did not). Thus there came a need to manage **dual distribution**, wherein different systems are used to reach each market segment efficiently and effectively. A firm's sales force served some segments; a distributor served others. This move away from only one method of going to market has accelerated. Now a firm may sell through retail outlets and via direct mail; use its own sales force to call on some accounts; rely on distributors to call smaller ones; and rely on other customers to find the company's 800 number or Web site, or to submit an order directly to the firm through some electronic data interchange system. In many firms, the economics of reaching the full set of its chosen target segments are such that a single approach for all customers simply won't work. Thus, rather than making one decision, the firm must make a coordinated set of decisions by market segment, recognizing and preparing to manage the conflicts that may arise across the different channel types.

In addition to customer requirements, the major considerations in channel length issues are:

- Account concentration: If a few customers represent the bulk of sales opportunities (e.g., jet engines), a direct selling approach can be cost effective. If the target group is larger in number and more diffuse (e.g., toothpaste), then the services of someone like a retailer who can spread the costs of an account relationship over many products is warranted.

- Degree of control and importance of direct customer contact: One reason to go direct may be the lack of intermediaries from whom the firm could secure adequate attention—that is, the firm lacks the power to gain some control over the intermediaries to ensure the necessary tasks are performed. Also, direct customer contact may be seen as a critical way to gain market understanding as an input into future product development efforts.

The second part of the channel design issue is channel breadth (i.e., how intense should the firm's presence be in a market area?). Does the firm wish to intensively distribute its product, making for maximal customer convenience (e.g., placing the product "within arm's reach of desire," as Coca-Cola terms it), or does it wish to be more selective? More selectivity may be warranted if there is a market education or development task to be done. Thus, some automobile manufacturers, typically high-end (e.g., Infiniti), limit the number of dealers in an area to reduce the dealer's concern that the benefits of developing potential customers in a given area would accrue to another dealer free-riding on these efforts.

In general, the strength of the argument for limiting distribution to selective or exclusive levels increases with:

- The customer's willingness to travel and search for the good

- The unit cost of stocking the good

- The amount of true "selling" or market development that must be done

As a product becomes more well known, there is a tendency to become less selective in distribution. For example, personal computers moved from computer specialty stores to mass merchants and warehouse clubs over time as customer education requirements decreased. Thus, the right channel structure changes over time. This presents a significant challenge as the firm seeks to maintain flexibility in channels while complex legal and other relationship elements tend to cement distribution arrangements.

Channel Management

Conflict between partners in a distribution system is not uncommon—more than a few litigations have been filed over issues like:

- "We provided a great product, but they never sold it the way they agreed to."

- "We developed the market, but they were never able to supply the product on a reliable basis."

- "They began distributing through a discounter right in the middle of the territory we spent years developing."

Many conflicts do not result in litigation but color the relationship—for example, a beer distributor lamenting, "Somehow their [the manufacturer's] view is that every time sales go up, it's their great advertising; when sales go down, it's our lousy sales promotion." In a general sense, all parties in the marketing system want the product to do well. But conflicts can arise from:

- Lack of congruence in goals—for example, the manufacturer's number one priority may be to "build the consumer franchise," while the distributor's is to make money this quarter

- Lack of consensus on who is doing what—for example, who is to perform certain functions such as after-the-sale service; who handles small accounts; who handles global or national accounts when assignments were originally made along a smaller geographic basis

Channel management is a day-to-day "work-on-it" task rather than a "solve-it-once" situation. Attention to proper design of contracts and other explicit understandings can help to reduce the potential for conflict. Good communications (for example, through dealer panels that are comprised of a sample of respondents from dealerships whose feedback is measured repeatedly over time) can help facilitate development of understanding and trust that will almost always be necessary to resolve issues since contracts cannot typically anticipate all the situations that may arise.

Promotion: Marketing Communications

The next element of the marketing mix is deciding the appropriate set of ways in which to communicate with customers to foster their awareness of the product, knowledge about its features, interest in purchasing, likelihood of trying the product and/or repeat purchasing it. Effective marketing requires an integrated communications plan combining both personal selling efforts and nonpersonal ones, such as advertising, sales promotion, and public relations.

Tasks and Tools

A useful mnemonic for the tasks in planning communications strategy is the six *M*s model:

1. Market: To whom is the communication to be addressed?

2. Mission: What is the objective of the communication?

3. Message: What are the specific points to be communicated?

4. Media: Which vehicles will be used to convey the message?

5. Money: How much will be spent in the effort?

6. Measurement: How will impact be assessed after the campaign?

The marketing communications mix is potentially extensive—for example, including nonpersonal elements (such as advertising, sales promotion events, direct marketing, public relations, packaging, and trade shows), as well as personal selling.[15]

A key to developing an effective communications strategy is understanding from the people involved in the purchase decision making of the roles they play and their current perceptions of the situation. Those involved, the so-called decision-making unit (DMU) for a product, can vary from very few (even just the user) to many. Hundreds may be involved in major industrial purchases.

Members of the DMU differ in the role played, their desires, and perhaps their perceptions; consequently, the need is for an integrated communications plan that uses different elements of the communications mix to address different issues pertinent to DMU members. Each element has particular strengths and weaknesses.

Nonpersonal Vehicles

Advertising in media is particularly effective in:

- Creating awareness of a new product

- Describing features of the product

- Suggesting usage situations

- Distinguishing the product from competitors

- Directing buyers to the point of purchase

- Creating or enhancing a brand image.

Advertising is limited in its ability to actually close the sale and make a transaction happen; sales promotions may be an effective device to complement the favorable attitude development for which advertising is appropriate.[16]

One trend in advertising is the movement to more precisely targeted media vehicles. For example, whereas the three major TV networks in the United States—namely ABC, CBS, and NBC—were once the only choices for television advertising, highly specialized channels like The Nashville Network (featuring country music) and the Golf Channel are now available through cable and satellite media. Direct marketing to households is another option. A direct mail piece can be customized to the household receiving it based on some demographic data available on mailing lists or even purchase histories. A catalog can both describe the firm's products and provide ordering information. Like a direct mail piece, the catalog can be customized to the household receiving it.

Sales promotions include things such as samples, coupons, and contests. These are usually most effective when used as a short-term inducement to generate action.

The three major types of sales promotions are:

1. Consumer promotions: used by a manufacturer and addressed to the end consumer—for example, a cents-off coupon sent in the mail or contained in print media or a continuity program such as collecting proofs of purchase to redeem for a gift

2. Trade promotions: used by the manufacturer and addressed to the trade—for example, temporary off-invoice price discounts or cooperative advertising allowances

3. Retail promotions: used by the trade and addressed to the end consumer (often this is stimulated by a trade promotion)—for example, offering a discount and displaying or advertising the brand[17]

Public relations refers to nonpaid communications efforts, such as press releases, speeches at industry seminars, or appearances by firm executives on radio or TV programs. These efforts do entail a cost to the firm but generally are distinguished from advertising by virtue of the fact that the firm does not pay for space in the media vehicle itself. For example, in some industries, new product reviews in the trade press are very influential with consumers. However, the output of public relations activities is somewhat less controllable than is the case with either advertising or sales promotion. Purchasing a TV spot pretty much guarantees that the firm's desires with respect to message and timing of delivery will be met. That level of control is not generally attainable with public relations since other parties decide whether or not to pick up a press release, write favorable or unfavorable things about the product in a review, and so forth.

Personal Selling

A salesperson as the communications vehicle presents the advantage of permitting an interaction to take place between the firm and a potential customer rather than just the broadcast of information. The salesperson can develop an understanding of the particular customer's perceptions and preferences and then tailor the communications message to the particulars of the situation. The importance of personal selling in the communications mix typically increases with the complexity of the product and the need for education of potential customers. For example, pharmaceutical companies maintain large field sales forces because nonpersonal media would not do an adequate job of educating doctors about new drugs.

It is critical to identify precisely the tasks of a salesperson. In some cases, the primary role is to take an order generated primarily by other elements of the marketing mix. In other cases, demand generation is a key task as the salesperson prospects for new accounts and/or performs consultative selling solving customers' problems. A salesperson can also have a role after the sale, providing technical support or transmitting customer data to the firm as a form of market research. Understanding the tasks to be done is a prerequisite to specifying skills and desired behaviors of salespeople. Recruiting, selecting, and training programs can be designed to provide the needed talents, and the evaluation, compensation, and motivation plans constructed to induce the necessary effort.

Constructing the Communications Mix

The proper allocation of dollars across the various media vehicles varies greatly depending upon the market situation. A fundamental decision is whether to focus on a push or pull strategy. In a **push strategy**, focus is on inducing intermediaries, such as a retailer, to sell the product at retail. Advertising's job may be to make the consumer aware of the product, but the closing of the deal is left to the intermediary. Alternatively, a **pull strategy** means the end consumer develops such an insistence on the product that the consumer "pulls" it through the channel of distribution, and the retailer's role is merely to make the product conveniently available.

As the number of feasible communications vehicles has increased (e.g., to event sponsorship, telemarketing, one's own Web site, a posting on someone else's Web site, and infomercials), the job of specifying the right communications mix has grown more complex simply due to the number of options and permutations and combinations to be considered. However, the growth in options also creates the possibility of gaining competitive advantage via superior performance in this task.

Pricing

To a large extent, the combination of product, place (channel), and promotion (communications mix) determine the target customer's perception of the value of the firm's product in a given competitive context. Conceptually, this perceived value represents the maximum price that the customer is willing to pay. This should be the primary guide to pricing the product. Once the firm has created value for customers, it is entitled to capture some of that value for itself to fund future value-creation efforts. This is the role of effective pricing.[18]

Pricing Basis and Objective

In most situations, cost should act as a floor on pricing. In some circumstances, a firm intentionally sells at a loss for a time to establish a position in the market, but it is often difficult to increase prices later due to the customer's use of the introductory price as a reference point.

With perceived value in mind, the first question is, what is the marketing objective, and how does the pricing objective derive from that? For example, the perceived value of the product typically varies by customer. Thus, the higher the price, the lower the sales rate, and vice versa. The price that would maximize short-term profit is thus typically higher than the one that would maximize market penetration, subject even to making some profit on each item.

Some have described this as a choice between a skim and a penetration pricing strategy. In a **skim strategy**, the focus is on those customers with high value—skimming the cream off the top of the market. The classic example of this is hardcover books at $30 initially for the impatient and dropping to $7 for the identical book in softcover about a year later. In **penetration pricing**, the firm sets a lower price to generate lots of sales quickly. This "leaves money on the table" with the high-value customers but is designed to preempt competition and gain a significant number of customers early on. The appeal of a penetration strategy increases to the extent that (1) customers are sensitive to price, (2) economies of scale are important, (3) adequate production capacity is available, and (4) there is a threat of competition.

Price Customization

Since customers typically place different values on the product, the firm should consider whether it is worth trying to capitalize on these value variations by charging different customers different prices. In some cases, legal constraints and logistical practicalities can make this infeasible. However, many firms owe their economic well-being to their ability to customize prices. For example, the yield management systems used by airlines and car rental companies have been a major source of profit, as prices are varied depending on when the buyer is booking, for how long, for which days of week, and so forth. These characteristics are used as indicators of the value the customer places on the product. Price customization can be achieved by:

- Developing a product line—such as the hardcover/softcover book situation just described

- Controlling the availability of lower prices—for example, by making them available only in certain locations

- Varying prices based on observable buyer characteristics—for example, software suppliers charge lower prices to "upgraders" than to new customers (the logic in new customers paying a higher price is they value the product more highly since they do not have the option of sticking with the current version; upgraders identify themselves by turning in some proof of ownership, such as support manuals)

• Varying prices based on observable characteristics of the transaction—for example, quantity discounts could be offered if the situation were that big-volume buyers valued the product less than small-volume buyers

Price Leadership

Some industries feature a large degree of pricing interdependence in an industry. That is, competitors react to pricing moves. Thus, any pricing decision has to reflect anticipated competitive reaction.

In some industries, legal and effective price leadership has been displayed as firms avoided price cutting in pursuit of share gains. In other industries, price wars have destroyed the profitability of nearly all the players. The tendency toward excessive price competition is particularly acute when:

• Firms have high fixed but low variable costs.

• There is little differentiation among competitors' products, and thus consumers largely buy on price.

• Industry growth rate is low.

• There are barriers to capacity adjustment, and economies of scale are important.

Thus, a key decision is how to ensure that the firm's actions do not have a negative impact on industry profitability by setting off a round of price cuts.

Analysis Underlying Marketing Strategy Formulation

As reflected at the top of figure 1-1, the major areas of analysis to be conducted in developing marketing strategy are the five *C*s:

1. Customers

2. Company

3. Competitors

4. Collaborators (e.g., channel partners and suppliers)

5. Context

Customer Analysis

Effective marketing requires in-depth understanding of customers' purchase and usage patterns. As noted earlier, an area to be considered is the decision-making unit:

- Who is involved in the process?

- What role does each play?

Researchers have identified five major roles in buying situations, and it should be understood who assumes each role (more than one individual can play each role, and one individual can play more than one role). These roles are:

- Initiator(s): recognize value in solving a particular issue and stimulate search for product

- Decider(s): make the choice

- Influencer(s): while not making the final decision, have input into it

- Purchaser(s): consummate the transaction

- User(s): consume the product

For example, in a decision to purchase a computer for the home, the initiator role may be held by the oldest child who saw value in it for a school assignments; the decider on brand was a relative with computer knowledge; parents and all children influenced the product features and price point; the purchaser was the same as the decider; and the user was all family members.

The second major area is the decision-making process:

- Is there a search for information?

- How is that search being conducted?

- What criteria are used to evaluate alternatives?

- How important are the various attributes, such as price and performance?

- How do DMU members interact?

Other considerations include:

- Where do customers wish to buy?

- How is the product to be used?

- How frequently/intently will it be used?

- How important is the problem that it solves?

These questions must be addressed at a disaggregate level so market segments can be identified.

Company Analysis

Corporate strengths and weaknesses must be understood since the fit of the product to the company is important as well as the fit to the market. Assessing product-company fit requires an understanding of the finances, R&D capability, manufacturing capability, and other assets of the firm.

Competitive Analysis

Marketers must identify both current and potential competitors. Competitors' strengths and weaknesses must be understood as the firm seeks differentiation possibilities. Similarly, in order to be able to predict and shape competitive reactions, the firm must assess competitors' objectives and strategies.

Collaborator Analysis

To the extent that there are important partners in the marketing system, their positions and goals must be assessed. Frequently, two key collaborators are the downstream trade (e.g., retailers) and upstream suppliers. With respect to the trade demand, the firm must understand their cost structure; expectations about margins and allocation of tasks; support and training requirements; and the nature of their relationship with the firm's competitors.

Increasingly, suppliers are being seen as critical collaborators in making marketing strategy work. What is their ability to supply quality product on a reliable basis? How much lead time is required, especially relative to the delivery time commitment to downstream customers?

Context Analysis

Marketing strategy can take very little for granted. The context shapes what is possible, and it is always changing. Indeed, spotting important changes in context before a competitor is a reliable path to competitive success. This point is vividly illustrated by the

Web's disruption of existing distribution and communication systems that generations of businesspeople took for granted. Clearly, then, marketing strategy analysis must be alert to technological context. What threats, vulnerabilities, opportunities, and resources does the technological frontier pose for the firm?

Culture, like technology, can shift and bring surprise unless carefully monitored. As many fortunes are made by anticipating cultural trends as technological trends, as Coca-Cola, McDonald's, and Nike attest. Products and services acquire meaning from their place in a culture, and they acquire economic value from that meaning. Value, then, is vulnerable to shifts in the culture (often called "trends" and "fashions"). The systematic analysis of cultural trends (popularized recently as "cool hunting" and "consumer ethnography") is increasingly an integral part of strategy formulation.

Similarly, politics, regulation, law, and social norms are not fixed features of the marketing landscape, but factors to consider and monitor for signs of disruption. Markets such as banking, television, and pharmaceuticals operate in particularly unstable settings. It is dangerous to design marketing strategy for such environments without a carefully developed point of view on the regulatory context.

The five Cs analysis is input into the construction of the marketing strategy. In the end, an economic analysis must be done to ensure that everything adds up to a viable business proposition. What are the fixed-dollar commitments? What level of unit contribution can be attained, and what is the anticipated associated sales level?

Summary

Devising an effective marketing program requires in-depth analysis to support decision making on a host of interrelated issues. Many books address this general topic and provide in-depth information on specific topics noted here.[19] This chapter's objective was to bring together the issues and analyses underlying marketing strategy development and to suggest resources that readers could consult if needed. It introduced five major areas of analysis underlying marketing decision making, namely the five *C*s—customers, company, competitors, collaborators, and context—and the core elements of the marketing mix, commonly called the four *P*s of product, price, promotion, and place. It noted a third useful mnemonic, the six *M*s, which relate to the tasks in planning communications strategy: market, mission, message, media, money, and measurement. The chapter concluded by returning to the five *C*s in terms of marketing strategy formulation.

Additional Readings on Marketing Strategy

Crittenden, Victoria L. "The Rebuilt Marketing Machine." *Business Horizons,* September 15, 2005. Based on a decade of company-based research, this article argues that marketing professionals must recognize and conceptualize their function as far more than just the four *P*s by addressing the key strategic issues that companies face in today's rapidly evolving, digitized marketplace.

Levitt, Theodore. "Marketing Myopia." *Harvard Business Review*, July 2004. First published in 1960, this classic article argues that organizations must learn to think of themselves not as producing goods or services but as doing the things that will make people want to do business with them; and the chief executives must create environments that support this mission.

McGovern, Gail J., et al. "Bringing Customers into the Boardroom." *Harvard Business Review*, November 2004. Misguided marketing strategies have destroyed more shareholder value than shoddy accounting or shady fiscal practices. This article presents a "marketing dashboard," a series of managerial reports that allows managers to assess quickly and routinely the effectiveness of their company's marketing strategies.

Notes

1. Summary was enhanced and Additional Readings were added to this chapter. They did not appear as such in the Class Note. The following

references appeared as footnotes in the Class Note but were lightly edited for consistency.

2. The idea for a chapter of this type as a useful adjunct to studying marketing originated with R. E. Corey, "Marketing Strategy: An Overview," Class Note 579-054 (Boston: Harvard Business School, 1978).

3. This chapter uses the term *product* although the logic conveyed applies equally to situations in which customer value is delivered by a product-service bundle or a service alone.

4. The development of customization strategies is covered in B. Joseph Pine II, *Mass Customization* (Boston: Harvard Business School Press, 1993), and D. Peppers and M. Rogers, *The One to One Future* (New York: Currency/Doubleday, 1993).

5. A good reference on the process of segmentation is in V. R. Rao and J. H. Steckel, "Segmenting Markets: Who Are the Potential Buyers?" *Analysis for Strategic Marketing* (Reading, MA: Addison-Wesley, 1998), ch. 2.

6. This conception of positioning has been popularized by A. Ries and J. Trout in *Positioning: The Battle for Your Mind*, revised 1st ed. (New York: McGraw-Hill, 2000).

7. P. Kotler and K. L. Keller, *Marketing Management: Analysis, Planning, Implementation and Control,* 12th ed. (Englewood Cliffs, NJ: Prentice Hall, 2005).

8. N. H. Borden, "The Concept of the Marketing Mix," reprinted in *Strategic Marketing Management*, ed. R. J. Dolan (Boston: Harvard Business School Press, 1991).

9. This example is offered by Regis McKenna as an illustration of an "integral product" in his "Marketing in an Age of Diversity," *Harvard Business Review*, September–October 1988.

10. These examples are offered and this topic is considered in detail in D. A. Aaker, *Managing Brand Equity* (New York: Free Press, 1991), particularly ch. 9.

11. This particular model is presented by G. C. Urban and J. R. Hauser in *Design and Marketing of New Products*, 2nd ed. (Englewood Cliffs, NJ: Prentice Hall, 1993).

12. These methods are described in C. M. Crawford, *New Product Management*, 5th ed. (Homewood, IL: Irwin, 1997), and R. J. Dolan, *Managing the New Product Development Process* (Reading, MA: Addison-Wesley, 1993).

13. V. K. Rangan, "Designing Channels of Distribution," Class Note 594-116 (Boston: Harvard Business School Publishing, 1994), also reprinted in V. K. Rangan, B. P. Shapiro, and R. T. Moriarty, *Business Marketing Strategy: Concepts and Applications* (Homewood, IL: Irwin, 1995).

14. This approach is advocated and described in detail in L. W. Stern, A. I. El-Answry, and A. T. Coughlan, *Marketing Channels*, 5th ed. (Englewood Cliffs, NJ: Prentice Hall, 1996), particularly ch. 5.

15. This categorization is given by P. W. Farris and J. A. Quelch in *Advertising and Promotion Management: A Manager's Guide to Theory and Practice* (Philadelphia: Chilton, 1983).

16. A good reference on advertising is D. A. Aaker, R. Batra, and J. G. Myers, *Advertising Management*, 4th ed. (Englewood Cliffs, NJ: Prentice Hall, 1992), wherein the need to consider advertising in the overall context of the communications mix is stressed.

17. R. C. Blattberg and S. A. Neslin, *Sales Promotion: Concepts, Methods, and Strategies* (Englewood Cliffs, NJ: Prentice Hall, 1990) uses this categorization. This book includes important information on the types and design of sales promotion events and empirical evidence on their impact.

18. This view is developed in R. J. Dolan and H. Simon, *Power Pricing* (New York: Free Press, 1996).

19. For general marketing management issues, good texts are T. K. Kinnear, K. L. Bernhardt, and K. A. Krentler, *Principles of Marketing*, 4th ed. (New York: HarperCollins, 1995), and Kotler and Keller, *Marketing Management*.

Basic Marketing Mathematics

THE CHAPTER "MARKETING STRATEGY" DESCRIBED
the scope of marketing analysis needed to provide the
basis for the development of a marketing strategy and the supporting
implementation plan.[1] The type of in-depth understanding of factors
described there is often usefully supplemented by numerical analysis;
at times, marketing practitioners need relatively complex, computer-
supported analysis. At others, a low-tech approach, utilizing the pro-
verbial "back of the envelope" and maybe a calculator, does the job.

This appendix defines key terms and basic calculations useful in
both problem analysis and real-life marketing decision making. To
accompany this knowledge, one needs to develop some intuition
about which type of numbers to look at when.

This appendix was written by Robert J. Dolan and originally published
as "Note on Low-Tech Marketing Math," Class Note 9-599-011 (Boston:
Harvard Business School Publishing, 1998). It was lightly edited for consistency.

Basic Terminology

Types of Cost

Most of the time, sellers hope to get a price that more than covers their cost. In other words, they try to make a profit. That profit is measured as the difference between the revenues taken in and the costs incurred.

It is often useful to make a distinction between two kinds of costs, fixed and variable. **Fixed costs** are those that remain at a given level regardless of the amount of the product produced and sold. An example of a fixed cost would be the firm's expenditure on an advertisement. Regardless of how much Budweiser beer or Nike athletic shoes are sold, the media outlet gets the same fee from the takers of its advertising time or space.

In contrast, **variable costs** are those that change depending upon the amount of product produced and sold. For example, the more beer Budweiser sells, the greater are its packaging costs, shipping costs, raw material costs, and so forth.

Marketers often look at the variable cost per unit, where the definition of "unit" matters. For example, the Sealed Air Corporation calculates the variable cost for a unit of its SD-120 product (where a *unit* is defined as a thousand square feet) to be $36.31—composed of two components, manufacturing ($28.38) and transportation ($7.93). Warner-Lambert Ireland pegs the company's variable cost for producing a fourteen-day supply of its Niconil product is £12 in Ireland.

In reality, the variable cost per unit may depend on the total output produced. In figure 1A-1, panels (a) and (b) present two different situations that arise.

In both panel (a) and panel (b), readers can see the fixed cost that is incurred regardless of volume produced. In panel (a), the total cost line, which is the sum of the fixed cost and total variable cost, is a straight line, meaning that it increases at a *constant* rate

FIGURE 1A-1

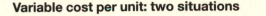

Variable cost per unit: two situations

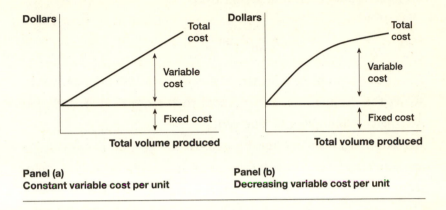

Panel (a)
Constant variable cost per unit

Panel (b)
Decreasing variable cost per unit

with increases in volume. This means the variable cost per unit is constant. Panel (b) shows the same fixed cost, but the shape of the total cost curve is different. It increases at a *decreasing* rate with volume. This means the variable cost per unit decreases the more the firm produces. This could happen for a number of reasons—for example, the firm gets more efficient in its manufacturing process or gets a better deal from raw material suppliers as it buys larger amounts from them. Most marketing case studies assume that panel (a) represents a reasonable approximation to the reality and take variable cost per unit to be a constant.

Margin Calculations

Sealed Air sells its SD-120 product for **$65.35** per unit. Marketers call the difference between the per unit revenue received by the firm and the variable cost per unit the **unit margin**. If it's clear from the context, marketers sometimes drop the *unit* part and simply call this *the margin*. Another term sometimes used to represent the same quantity is *unit contribution*. One can calculate Sealed Air's margin as **$65.35 – $36.31 = $29.04**.

Sometimes, it is useful to state the margin in percentage terms. To get this, divide the unit margin in dollars by the revenue per unit. For example, for Sealed Air, this is:

$$\frac{29.04}{\$65.35} = .444$$

To put this in percentage terms, multiply by 100; in other words, swing the decimal point two places to the right—that is, Sealed Air's percent margin is 44.4 percent.

Note that in calculating the percent margin, do not divide by the firm's cost, but rather by the revenue it receives. This is something one has to be careful about. For example, consider a retailer that gets a 50 percent margin on jewelry. For an item that costs the retailer $100, this means the selling price is $200. This situation is shown in figure 1A-2:

The percent margin is defined by (A) ÷ (C), not (A) ÷ (B).

Given this, you figure a **selling price** given a cost and a percent margin like this (the derivation of this calculation appears at the end of this appendix):

FIGURE 1A-2

Calculating the percent margin

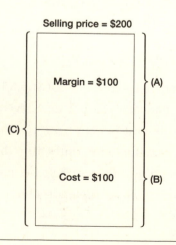

$$Selling\ Price = \frac{Cost}{1 - [Percent\ Margin/100]}$$

Marketers sometimes look at the margin structure for a channel of distribution. For example, consider figure 1A-3, which shows the channel for a producer or manufacturer of the *Beginning to Golf* instruction tape.

The manufacturer sells through a wholesaler, who in turns sells to retailers, who then sell to the public. Each of the three members of the channel of distribution (manufacturer, wholesaler, retailer) performs a function and is compensated for it by the margin that member receives (see figure 1A-4).

FIGURE 1A-3

Price and cost at levels in the channel of distribution

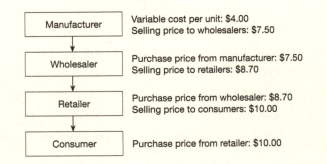

Manufacturer	Variable cost per unit: $4.00 Selling price to wholesalers: $7.50
Wholesaler	Purchase price from manufacturer: $7.50 Selling price to retailers: $8.70
Retailer	Purchase price from wholesaler: $8.70 Selling price to consumers: $10.00
Consumer	Purchase price from retailer: $10.00

FIGURE 1A-4

Margins for three channels of distribution

Manufacturer's margin ($3.50)	=	Manufacturer's selling price to distributors ($7.50)	−	Manufacturing cost ($4.00)
Wholesaler's margin ($1.20)	=	Wholesaler's selling price to retailers ($8.70)	−	Price paid to manufacturer ($7.50)
Retailer's margin ($1.30)	=	Retailer's selling price to consumers ($10.00)	−	Price paid to wholesaler ($8.70)

So the dollar margin is a measure of how much each organization makes per unit sold.

In this example, the retailer's percent margin is 13 percent ($1.30 on the retailer's $10 selling price to consumers). The manufacturer's and wholesaler's percent margins are 46.67 percent and 13.79 percent, respectively.

Break-Evens

Recovering Fixed Costs

What the organization makes in margins helps it to cover its fixed costs and hopefully produce a profit. The number of units sold that just enables the company to cover its fixed costs is its **break-even volume** (BEV). Mathematically, this BEV is given by:

$$BEV = \frac{Fixed\ Costs\ in\ Dollars}{Dollar\ Margin\ Per\ Unit}$$

For example, say the *Beginning to Golf* tape manufacturer had **$700,000** in costs to produce the tape. These costs are fixed because they would not change with the number of tapes sold. Given the **$3.50** margin per tape, to recover the **$700,000** investment, the manufacturer would have to sell the break-even volume of:

$$BEV = \frac{\$700,000}{\$3.50/unit} = 200,000\ units$$

Changes in Fixed Cost

One can also use this type of calculation to see what other potential investments would have to yield to be worthwhile. For example, suppose a noted golf pro will endorse the tapes for a one-time payment of **$175,000**. This would be worthwhile if the manufacturer believed that the endorsement would result in added sales of:

$$\frac{Added\ Costs}{Dollar\ Margin\ Per\ Unit} = \frac{\$175,000}{\$3.50/unit} = 50,000\ units$$

Changes in Margin Per Unit

Similarly, one can examine the impact of changes in the unit margin. Suppose the noted golf professional did not require a $175,000 fixed payment for the endorsement but instead wanted a $1 royalty per tape sold. This would cut the manufacturer's margin from $3.50 to $2.50 per tape. The change in the break-even volume could then be assessed by:

$$BEV = \frac{\$700,000}{\$2.50/unit} = 280,000\ units$$

This represents a 40 percent increase in the break-even volume from 200,000 units with no endorsement.

Market Size and Share

One would have to know a lot more about the market and the quality of the products before any decisions could be made using these numbers. That is, the 200,000 units required to break even (assuming the manufacturer opted against using the endorsement) may be a "big number" for the firm, or it may be easily attainable for the firm. All the factors set out in the chapter on marketing strategy have to be assessed to determine that.

In conjunction with that, it is sometimes useful to convert the break-even units number into a **share of market** number. For example, suppose that some research showed that a total of **5,000,000** golf instruction videos were likely to be sold annually. Then, one could calculate the break-even market share:

$$Break\text{-}Even\ Share\ of\ Golf\ Video\ Market = \frac{200,000\ units}{5,000,000\ units} = 4\%$$

This might yield added insight. Note however that how to define "the market" is a question to consider.

Suppose research further showed that of the 5,000,000 tapes sold, only **1,000,000** were of the beginner variety. It might be more appropriate to look at the share needed of this market, that is:

$$\textit{Break-Even Share of Golf Video Market} = \frac{200,000 \ units}{1,000,000 \ units} = 20\%$$

One also needs to select the most appropriate time horizon. This will vary with the specific situation. The two share figures calculated here implicitly assumed that the manufacturer was looking to recover its fixed costs in one year.

Impact of Price Decisions

Figure 1A-5 shows the drivers of profit. To this point, this discussion has largely focused on the right-hand branch of this profit tree. Simple calculations also can help in assessing price decisions shown on the left-hand branch.

FIGURE 1A-5

Profit drivers

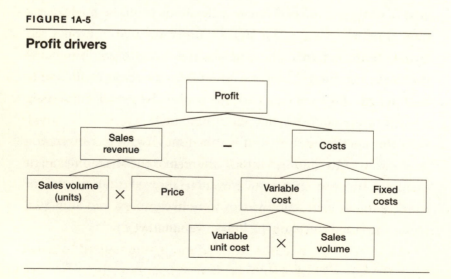

Consider a manufacturer selling at $100 per unit and achieving sales of 1 million units per year. Assuming the variable cost per unit is $60, the manufacturer's unit margin is $40. Panel (a) of figure 1A-6 shows this situation. The shaded rectangle represents the total margin of $40 million (1 million total units multiplied by a $40 unit margin). The total contribution or margin can always be represented as a rectangle on a price and unit volume graph since it is the product of the unit margin (rectangle width) and sales volume in units (rectangle height).

Suppose management questioned whether the current $100 price yielded the highest possible total margin and was considering alternative prices in the range of plus or minus 20 percent from the current price. As a first step, one might want to know the unit sales volume required to maintain the $40 million total margin with alternative prices.

Consider the 20 percent price cut alternative as shown in panel (b) of figure 1A-6. An $80 price with unchanged variable unit cost of $60 reduces the unit margin from $40 to $20. Thus, the company now has to sell twice as many units as it did at a price of $100 to achieve the same total margin and profit. With 2 million units sold at $80, sales revenue would increase to $160 million, but the total margin remains at $40 million. Since the total margin is unchanged, the area of the shaded rectangle is the same as in panel (a). While the price reduction is only 20 percent, the reduction in unit margin is 50 percent. The sales increase required to compensate for this smaller margin accordingly is 100 percent. One can always think of the volume adjustment needed to keep contribution the same as a problem of keeping the area of the shaded rectangle the same. As the price decreases, the rectangle gets thinner and so must get taller. As the price increases, the rectangle gets fatter and hence can get shorter and still have the same area.

The 20 percent price-increase scenario is summarized in panel (c) of the figure. With a $120 price, unit margin increases to $60,

Effect of price on total margin

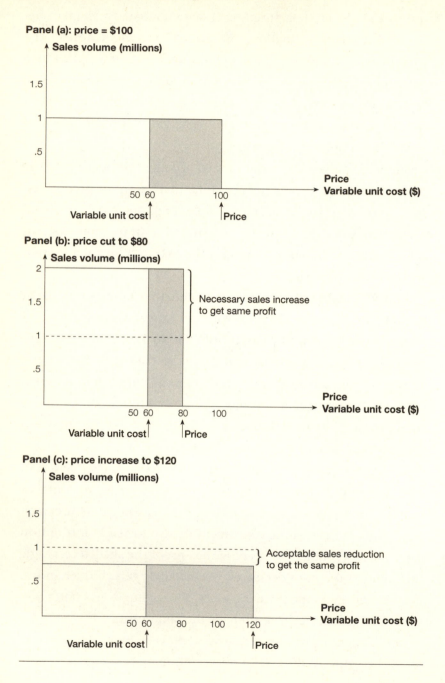

thereby requiring only 666,666 units to be sold to generate $40 million total margin. Thus, a 33.3 percent decrease in volume will leave the total margin unchanged. If unit sales decline by less than 33.3 percent, the price increase would drive the total margin and profit up.

As one can see, price decreases and increases have highly leveraged effects. A seemingly small reduction in price can have a large negative impact on unit contribution, requiring a tremendous increase in sales volume to generate the same profit. A small percentage price increase can have a strong positive effect on unit margin, creating a large, acceptable decrease in sales volume while still retaining the margin level. These effects are most pronounced when variable costs are high and unit margins small.

Using the Numbers

This appendix has shown how one can calculate a quantity given other quantities. Essentially, it's shown how to translate some facts or estimates into other facts/estimates. This translation process is useful if the end result is an accurately derived fact/estimate that is suggestive of what one should do as a manager.

The key point is this: numbers often become significant in an argument when there is some benchmark to compare them to. In marketing, such benchmarks are developed from understanding the market size, growth rate, and competitive activity. Calculations in and of themselves are useless unless combined with other information to provide a meaningful context.

As noted at the outset, useful numbers work requires intuition about what quantities to calculate. That intuition will develop through practice on bringing numbers to bear on arguments in a well-connected way. This short appendix does little to develop that intuition. The goals here were more modest—that is, to specify terminology and mechanics, and to suggest potential applications.

Derivation of the Formula for Price

Suppose a firm's unit cost is **C** and its percent margin is **M**. Let **P** equal the price it receives. By definition of the percent margin, one knows:

$$[M/100] = \frac{P - C}{P} \tag{1}$$

To solve equation (1) for **P**, first multiply both sides of (1) by **P** to get:

$$P[M/100] = P - C \tag{2}$$

Subtract **P** from both sides:

$$P[M/100] - P = -C \tag{3}$$

Factor out the **P** on the left-hand side:

$$P[M/100 - 1] = -C \tag{4}$$

Multiply both sides by: $\dfrac{-1}{[M/100 - 1]}$

$$P = \frac{C}{[1 - M/100]} \tag{5}$$

Example: a firm's cost is $25 and it wants to make a percent margin of 40 percent (**M** = 40). Therefore, its price has to be:

$$\frac{\$25}{1 - 40/100} = \frac{25}{.6} = \$41.66$$

To check: at **$41.66**, the margin is $41.66 − $25 = $16.66. Thus, the percent margin is ($16.66/$41.66) × 100 = 40% as required.

The goal of the quantitative analysis must always be kept clear: to help in making marketing policy decisions.

Notes

1. Professor Luc Wathieu provided helpful comments and input on the original note. It was prepared for class discussion rather than to illustrate either effective or ineffective handling of an administrative situation.

Understanding Consumer Behavior

ORGANIZATIONS SUCCEED BECAUSE OF THEIR ability to satisfy outside clients for their goods and services.[1] This ability depends on how well organizations understand their clients and use these insights effectively. Ultimately, the competitive advantage one firm has over another stems from its superior understanding of its customers *and* a superior process for thinking about and acting on this information.

This chapter introduces concepts that help in understanding clients, traditionally called "customers" or "buyers." These concepts are also relevant to other kinds of clients such as voters, museum and symphony patrons, recipients of government services, and beneficiaries of social causes. This chapter begins with a discussion of the centrality of the customer to the firm and marketing's special role with respect to the customer.

This chapter was written by Gerald Zaltman and originally published as "Note on Consumer Behavior," Class Note 9-597-057 (Boston: Harvard Business School Publishing, 1997). It was edited for consistency.

Marketing's Customer Focus

Marketing is the process of planning and executing the development, pricing, promotion, and distribution of ideas, goods, and services *to create exchanges* that satisfy individual and organizational objectives. The definition of marketing as an exchange process makes the understanding, predicting, and influencing of customers the unique and central task of the marketing function and sensitizes practitioners to four fundamental objectives:

1. To ensure that customers understand the basic concept behind a product or service

2. To show customers the relevance of the firm's product or service to their needs

3. To remove or lower barriers to exchange so that customers can engage in a transaction with minimal effort

4. To develop and manage trustworthy relationships with customers, thereby providing the context in which exchanges occur

The "voice" of the customer must be heard throughout the organization since nearly all decisions in a firm directly or indirectly affect those objectives. For instance, decisions on return on investment criteria and senior management's decisions based on their understanding of competitors and regulatory agencies may influence which products are introduced and withdrawn from the marketplace. Decisions made by managers in human resources, manufacturing, shipping, and R&D may affect both the real and perceived quality of goods and services. Thus, managers throughout the organization must understand what customers want and will pay for, and must apply this information creatively in their decision making.

The marketing function affects customers more directly than any other single area of the firm. However, beyond its own significant decisions about pricing, product offerings, promotion, and distribution, marketing is responsible for helping other functions understand their effect on customers. Marketing, then, which generally understands customers best, must lead in making the entire firm customer oriented.

Why Understanding Customers Is Important

Today, the half-life of knowledge about the marketplace is getting shorter and shorter. That is, rapid social and technological changes are shrinking the period of time for which existing understandings and predictions about the marketplace are valid. Even using one's knowledge of customers creates changes in the marketplace, which may lessen the validity of the knowledge originally acted on. Therefore, managers must update and reexamine existing conceptions, predictions, and assumptions about customers more frequently than ever before.

Managers require deeper and richer understandings of customers to anticipate or predict and even shape behavior, and they need better methods for collecting insights about customers and better ways of thinking about these insights to lessen certain errors common among them when they think about customers. For example, managers sometimes assume that:

- Their own personal experiences represent a larger market.

- They can treat changes in customer behavior as isolated events rather than as part of a complex system of events.

- Research methods and thinking frameworks that have proved useful in the past are appropriate in the present.

- Customers know why their behavior has changed, and so the "data speaks for itself."

- They need not develop basic understandings of why people behave as they do to predict accurately what they will do in

a complex, changing environment (where short-term thinking leads to even shorter-lived success).

The U.S. auto industry illustrates the social and economic costs
of losing touch with the voice of the customer. This widely studied
industry also typifies what is happening now in many firms in many
industries around the world. While many factors contributed to
the decline and emerging turnaround of this industry, one stands
out above all others. Basically, there was a failure to: (1) anticipate
the possibility of change among customers, (2) detect important
changes soon after they occurred, (3) understand these changes
once they became painfully evident, and (4) integrate the voice of
the customer in key decisions once that voice was understood.

Well-educated, hardworking, and dedicated managers commit-
ted these errors. They displayed two fundamental, related decision-making biases. First, they assumed that what had worked well
in the past would continue to work in the future, often called the
"failure of success bias." Second, they failed to develop wide cognitive peripheral vision: they failed to perceive the relevance of
changes in customer thinking and behavior before their competitors did. Their narrow cognitive peripheral vision was partly a failure in imagination.

Customer Behavior Defined

The complexity and fascination of human behavior is nowhere more
evident than when people make and implement purchase decisions and engage in consumption and postconsumption activities.
Customer behavior is the outcropping of cognitive processes, social
interactions, and the functioning of social institutions. Concepts
and research in the humanities and various social and biological
sciences can enlighten a firm's understanding of customers and
hence its ability to anticipate and shape customers' behaviors.[2]

The deeper this understanding, the greater the opportunity to anticipate and shape customer behavior and to gain competitive advantage. For instance, knowledge of cognitive processes that "unpack" information in an advertisement or the design of an automobile can improve the design of advertising and products. This requires marketing practitioners to understand the commonly perceived or socially shared symbolism of particular advertising cues and product features as well as the social processes and institutions whereby this symbolism acquires common meaning for a market segment. Thus, when approached in the most constructive way possible, the study of customers is also an exploration of fundamental human behavior. The use of mathematics and statistics is an important part of this exploration and is particularly useful for predicting behavior.

Customer behavior consists of the acts, processes, and social relationships displayed by individuals or groups before, during, and subsequent to an exchange process. Four comingling phenomena characterize customer behavior: (1) *people*, including individuals and informal and formal groups of varying sizes, (2) engaging in *activities*, including actions and processes, (3) in the context of interpersonal *relationships*, (4) which create *experiences*, including those associated with obtaining, using, and dealing with the consequences of goods and services.

For example, while enacting the role of a medical patient, an individual may seek word-of-mouth information (a communication process) from other people (involving social relationships) about medical services. This may lead to a medical consultation, involving a new relationship with a physician or even a formal group such as an HMO. The consumer obtains advice that is presumably used and may require obtaining other products and services, with a subsequent improvement, or conceivably a deterioration, in health. Satisfaction or dissatisfaction with the medical service is another consequence.

Customer behavior may be displayed by a committee, often called a "buying center."

Unit of Analysis

An important aspect of customer behavior deserves special emphasis: customer behavior is social in nature. Because marketing practitioners often collect data from individuals, they tend to underestimate the impact of other people, social institutions, and social settings on those individuals. However, customers can only be understood well in terms of their relationships with other people and in terms of their larger social context. Thus the first step in any study of customer behavior is to define the unit(s) of analysis (i.e., who or what one is trying to understand or explain). The discussion that follows addresses just a few of the many units of analysis of interest to marketers.

Types of Customers

A distinction is often made between two general units of analysis: the ultimate consumer and the formal organization. Despite important differences, the two units also share much in common, and the distinction is sometimes one of convenience. A brief overview will be helpful.

A customer may be a household or an organization in an industrial market. In either case, it may be a single person or a collection of people, as shown in figure 2-1. Most research addresses individual decision makers (cell 1). Customers often are multiperson decision-making units, however. In families (cell 2), different people may be involved at different stages of the decision-making process or have different kinds and degrees of influence in the decision. One person may control the information to be used. Others may decide which product is most appropriate, finance the purchase, buy the product, or use it. Thus, different family members may play different roles in the buying process. This also creates the potential for conflict since multiple needs must be satisfied.

FIGURE 2-1

Types of customers

	Individual	Group
Household	**Cell 1** Individual buying	**Cell 2** Family buying unit
Organization	**Cell 4** The organizational buyer (e.g, the purchasing agent)	**Cell 3** The buying center

People involved in the buying process in organizations are often referred to as the "buying center" (cell 3) because the buying process often transcends departmental lines. The purchase of capital equipment, for example, might include the purchasing agent, an engineer, a senior financial officer, and outside consultants. Generally, the more important, risky, or expensive the product or the service, the greater the number of people in the buying center. Again, as with families, different members play different roles in the buying process, and these roles vary with different purchases. Different needs among buying-center members also raise the potential for conflict between them. In other cases (cell 4) organizational buying is conducted by a single individual such as a purchasing agent.

Some consumer and organizational buying processes are similar, especially in small businesses. Still, many aspects of organizational (or industrial) buying are distinct enough to have received special attention in models of organizational buying behavior. These are discussed in the box, "How the Type of Decision Affects the Decision-Making Process."

How the Type of Decision Affects the Decision-Making Process

One variable in such buying models is the task or nature of the problem to be solved. The problem can be quite routine, requiring a straightforward reordering of the same product from the same supplier; it may be nonroutine and involve substantial information processing about products and suppliers; or it may fall somewhere in between in what is called a "modified rebuy." The less routine a problem is, the larger the number of people usually involved in the decision process. The larger the number of people and the more diverse the areas of the firm they represent, the longer the time required to develop a choice. In a family decision setting the number of people involved in a decision and who they are is usually fixed.

The different buying situations tend to involve different processes or enactment of different decision-making activities. For example, the following sets of decisions are made by buying centers:

- The anticipation or identification of a problem or need

- Determining what kind of solution would be appropriate (i.e., what characterizes an effective purchase)

- Identification of potential vendors

- Solicitation of proposals or bids

- Evaluation of proposals and selection of a supplier

- Evaluation of the product or service

The way in which these and other decisions are made will vary depending on whether customers are in a new task-buying situation requiring extensive problem solving and thus more time in activities 1 and 2; a straight rebuy situation where the problem is a continuing one requiring simple routine actions; or a modified rebuy situation involving limited problem solving where customers may know what they want but may be unsure of the best source of supply and thus more time is spent in activities 3 and 5.

Generally, when more people are involved in a decision, the dynamics of these activities change. For instance, when personnel from several areas of a company are involved in the buying center, there may be more time spent resolving conflicts. Conflicts may arise when different perspectives (usually corresponding to different functional areas and kinds of expertise) result in different definitions of the problem and of the solution. There may also be different interpretations of information intended to help define the problem and to create or find a solution. Conflict resolution thus becomes a distinctive activity, especially in a nonroutine purchase decision. Even so, such differences in judgment can be very healthy and even essential to developing successful choices. Different perspectives add new insights and help guard against the automatic use of decision rules—or habits of mind— that have worked in the past but may be inappropriate now.

One well-known model, the **Webster and Wind model**, stresses four sets of forces that shape organizational buying behavior. First, there are the internal social relationships among members of the buying center, including how often they work together in a buying center, how much trust has developed, and so forth. Recent research addresses such issues as bargaining, negotiation, conflict, the use of power and other influence strategies, and so on among members of buying centers. Second, there are the special qualities of each person in the buying center. These qualities include their skills, access to information sources, how they process information, and their style of work-

(continued)

ing with others. Third, there are organizational factors such as how centralized, formal, and complex a firm is and what its goals and distinctive competencies and limitations are. Also important is how the responsibilities of the buying center are structured. Broadly speaking, this includes such matters as who it reports to, how its tasks are distributed among members, how much power or authority it has (whether it recommends to others or actually implements its choices), how the center is organized, whether its members come from different areas of the firm and from the same or different levels of authority within the firm, and the authority of its leader. Finally, there are forces in the external environment of the firm that present both opportunities and constraints. For example, if continuity of supply of critical parts is a potential problem, the firm may wish to subsidize certain suppliers, even if they are more costly sources, as a way of ensuring long-term product availability.

These and many other forces interact. For example, the size of the firm, its complexity, and other structural characteristics may influence how the buying center is organized—that is, how many people are involved, from which levels and areas of the firm they come from, what their responsibilities are, and how influential the buying center leader is. Moreover, the nature of the task is critical. This includes such factors as the importance of the purchase, how new or novel it is, and how difficult or complex the purchase is. If a purchase is technically complex or has a wide impact within the firm, many different perspectives or kinds of expertise may be required resulting in the involvement of many different functions. If the purchase is one with which the firm has little prior experience, there may be a very clear division of responsibility within the buying center.

Key Roles

There are a variety of key roles among customers. Among ultimate consumers these roles may be occupied by different people, although a person can engage in more than one role. Similarly, different firms may play one or more of these roles within an industry:

- Opinion leaders: People whose judgment or expertise is valued and sought by many others, usually with respect to a specific product category such as home appliances or financial planning.

- Market mavens: People who are knowledgeable about buying strategies generally and can provide broad or cross-category advice about shopping and where or how to get information. There is only a modest correlation or overlap between market mavens and opinion leaders.

- Innovators: People who are among the very first to try a product or service they perceive as new or novel. Innovators are influential because others often rely on the experience of innovators to anticipate their own experience with the new product or service. Opinion leaders watch innovators closely. There is only a modest overlap between innovators and opinion leaders and market mavens. Very few people will score highly on measures of all three attributes.

- Gatekeepers: People such as opinion leaders and market mavens who control enough of a channel of communication so as to influence what information flows to others and how quickly. However, gatekeepers need not be specialists about products or buying strategies. They need only occupy a strategic role in a channel of communication.

- Decision makers: People who formally "make" and authorize a purchase decision.

- Implementers: People who execute on a decision. Sometimes, decision makers only authorize purchase in a category; others, such as a purchasing agent or other intermediary, must select a specific brand or supplier.

- Users: People who directly experience the consumption of goods and services. This role sometimes includes anyone affected by another's use of a product or service.

Another important role involves **marketers**. For example, since marketing is an exchange process, there can be no "buyer" without a "seller" and, of course, vice versa. Moreover, both parties to the exchange process are both buying and selling—that is, each is giving and getting something of value. So, while it is often convenient to focus just on the behavior of customers or just on that of managers and their organizations, an important unit of analysis is also the **buyer-seller dyad** or the relationship between buyers and sellers. For instance, one may collect data from customers in a test of alternative advertising cues, but one is also asking customers to respond to stimuli reflecting certain beliefs among marketing specialists about these customers and about the meaning of the product or service. The seller can't avoid a presence in the customer's mind and vice versa. Each party has thoughts and actions that shape and are shaped by the other. Thus, the dyad may be the most fundamental or core unit of analysis. Viewed in this way, the marketing manager becomes a manager of relationships with customers. This is consistent with the view of marketing as the interface function between the firm and its customers.

One implication of these ideas about key roles is that the most effective way to gain a favorable purchase decision outcome often may not be to target users or decision makers directly, but rather to target those who determine what information decision makers receive and when, how decision makers evaluate information, and how those decisions are put into effect. In fact, communications research shows that decision makers among ultimate consumers and within organizations are typically more influenced by information reaching them through a social network than when received directly from sellers. This is true even when the essential information is supplied by sellers. Thus, managers must understand the dynamics of these roles—that is, who talks to whom, when, why, and with what effect. This may seem counterintuitive since mass-media advertising and direct mail can sometimes have an immediate effect on sales. However, even these seemingly immediate effects occur within a decision-making context already substantially influenced by past relationships, social processes, and prior experience. That is, the effects of marketer-controlled communications on individuals are mediated by social and cultural processes. However, because marketer-controlled communications are much more visible, people tend to overemphasize those communications' direct impact on customers.

The focus on key roles and social context is consistent with the concept of a multistep flow of influence versus a single or hypodermic needle viewpoint. It is also consistent with the trend in both communication theory and practice to view communication less as a linear, one-way process and more as a symmetric process whereby two or more parties interact to develop shared beliefs. The growth of interactive and other communications technologies, the greater speed with which market information is collected and acted upon, and other developments are making the traditional view of communication as a one-way process less useful.

Modeling Customer Behavior

The complexity of consumer behavior has led researchers to develop general models of customer behavior, which are simplifications that help organize thinking about customers. The earlier discussion of the buying center drew upon some of these models.

FIGURE 2-2

Past, present, and future social events

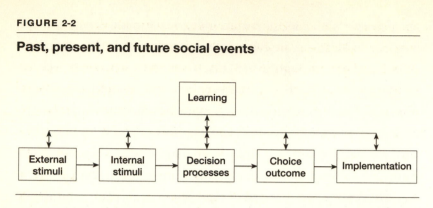

Various models, often presented as flow charts, share certain features, as shown in figure 2-2. This figure must be viewed within an enormously complex context of past, present, and future social events.

Different models usually show a set of external stimuli such as a sales call, exposure to a novel product design at a trade show, or an upcoming occasion requiring the giving of a gift. Thus an **external stimulus** is an actual or anticipated change in the environment that might be perceived by the decision-making unit. If salient enough, these stimuli may create a state of arousal for the decision-making unit. There are also **internal stimuli**, such as an inventory of component parts falling below a certain level, a change in financial circumstances, or being hungry. These, too, may create a state of arousal. Other internal stimuli may involve thoughts and feelings such as being bored or wanting to be like (or unlike) other people. Internal stimuli also include the requirements of various social roles people occupy and how people conceptualize problems, memories, and so forth.

External and internal stimuli register via multiple perceptual and sensing processes that are critical internal mechanisms for both individuals and organizations. Consumers can only know their environment by processing information provided initially by their senses. Similarly, organizations have various information systems for collecting data about their environments. Once data is acquired and the motivation to act is developed, a variety of decision processes occur. There are many widely studied decision-process topics, such as the development of attitudes, information-processing heuristics (rules of thumb), and the adoption of innovations. These and other important processes are guided by a variety of factors such as what people have learned from their own or others' experiences and their own feelings, preferences, goals, and thinking styles.

The decision process results in a **choice outcome**, an intention to purchase a product or service. The choice outcome may be at the product-category level only, such as the decision to purchase an automobile, or at the nameplate level, such as a decision to purchase a specific model, like a Buick. The intent to purchase requires implementation. Implementation may be quite simple, such as automatic reordering, or quite complex and time consuming. It may or may not be a pleasant experience. While not discussed here, the implementation of an intent to purchase can be sufficiently challenging that many people do not follow through.

Choice outcomes may also include the decision to not purchase or to defer further consideration pending the acquisition of more information, added resources, or better choice options. Whether or not a decision to buy is made and implemented, customers learn from their choices. This learning will affect their attention to and subsequent use of external and internal stimuli in future decision processes.

The categories shown in figure 2-2 are very broad, and the boundaries between them not always clear. For example, decision makers may adopt criteria used by *Consumer Reports* (an external stimulus) for, say, air conditioners, as their own personal choice criteria. Indeed, people may go directly from this or another external source of expertise, such as an opinion leader or market maven, to the choice of a specific brand of air conditioner with little other processing of information. Sometimes, too, a choice outcome is the starting point in the process shown in figure 2-2. An example would be receiving a gift or trial subscription to a magazine.

Like all models, figure 2-2 inadvertently emphasizes certain things, such as the individual and linearity of thinking, and de-emphasizes other things, such as culture and the impact of actions by the firm or other groups on customers. Furthermore, the overall process may vary according to different social roles, such as innovators and gatekeepers. Innovators could spend more time at the decision-making stage whereas gatekeepers could spend more time processing external stimuli. Moreover, what each does at these stages may differ.

The fact that customers may vary in how they enact the process shown in figure 2-2 is reflected by four types of problem-solving behavior: extensive, limited, routinized, and exploratory problem solving.

Extensive Problem-Solving Behavior

Extensive problem solving is likely to occur when the customer is purchasing a product new to the customer and has little prior knowledge about available products and how each should be evaluated. Under these circumstances the customer is likely to feel the need to process large amounts of product information. An example would be the first-time purchase of a computer. The customer is therefore highly involved in information-search and information-processing activities.

Similarly, when an organization is faced with the task of buying a new type of product, it often engages in extensive problem solving, particularly if the risk of a bad choice is rather high. The buying committee frequently initiates a rather extensive search for information and engages in a thorough analysis of alternatives to lessen the risk of choosing the wrong product or supplier. Individuals from several functional areas are likely to be involved. This increases the variety of information potentially available since different functional areas have access to different external and internal sources of information.

Limited Problem-Solving Behavior

Limited problem solving occurs when more product knowledge is available, perhaps because the customer has some limited experience with the product. The purchasing agent who has had some experience with heavy-duty air tools may already know what attributes are important and may need only focus on information about those attributes.

Routinized Problem-Solving Behavior

When consumers have had extensive experience purchasing the same product and are highly satisfied with it, their behavior becomes routinized. In organizational buying, continued and sustained purchase of the same product is called a **straight rebuy**. Decision-making efforts involved in purchasing are minimal. Customers already are confident that they are purchasing the best product available and feel no need to consider alternatives. They are said to be brand loyal.

In routinized buying situations customers may simply rely on package design, logos, or similar cues when taking the preferred brand from among alternatives on the shelf in a retail store. They are not likely to engage in postpurchase evaluation. In an organizational setting, the straight rebuy involves products from suppliers who have satisfactorily delivered the same product previously. Decision-making processes are likely to involve only one person or a very few people and are likely to be made quickly.

Exploratory Problem-Solving Behavior

After considerable experience with a single brand, customers may feel the need to reevaluate their purchase decision. This can result in exploratory purchasing. Customers may simply be tired of the brand they buy and wish to switch to an alternative. Or marketplace conditions may have changed and new or modified products may have appeared that are superior to the brand usually purchased. The customer may thus feel the need to reenter the market and reevaluate the appropriateness of the customer's current brand. Exploratory purchase is likely to occur when products are sensory in nature (e.g., food and drinks) or are in highly technical markets where improvements in the product can take place over short periods of time.

Forming Attitudes

Attitudes are general evaluations of a brand or product that are based on information and experience. They are carried in memory and help customers to differentiate offerings into acceptable and unacceptable sets. When attitudes do not exist in memory, customers attempt to form them.

One model of attitude formation and change that has gained considerable popularity in marketing is **Fishbein's multiattribute attitude model**.[3] According to this model, customers first generate a set of salient (or important) beliefs about a brand based on external and/or internal stimuli. As part of the decision process a probability is assigned to each belief statement, reflecting the customer's degree of certainty that the brand has that attribute. Each belief is also evaluated in terms of the customer's preferences.

In effect, the belief strength and the evaluation for each of the attributes are multiplied together. That is, it is *as if* customers do this. The belief-evaluation outcomes for each attribute are then to-

FIGURE 2-3

Fishbein's multiattribute attitude model

$$A_o = \sum_{i=1}^{n} b_i e_i$$

where:

A_o = attitude toward the object
b_i = belief strength assigned to a particular attribute
e_i = evaluation assigned to a particular attribute

$\sum_{i=1}^{n}$ = summation of all the product attributes (1 to n)

taled to form the attitude. The formal statement for this set of mathematical operations is shown in figure 2-3.

This model has fairly high levels of predictive validity. It is interesting to marketers because it suggests not only how attitudes are formed but also how marketers may change customers' attitudes by one of the following means:

- Change the types of beliefs that make up the relevant set— for example, make certain attributes more salient than others

- Change the probability value that customers assign to various beliefs—that is, increase the probability value associated with a positive evaluated belief and decrease the probability value associated with a negative evaluated belief

- Change the customers' evaluations of the various attributes— that is, make a previously negative attribute seem positive

Most research on how customers develop brand preferences and make choices has focused on products with tangible attributes. Typical research might focus on how people evaluate laundry appliances based on such obvious features as cost, speed, warranty, and load capacity. Less attention has been given to products with abstract concepts. For a symbolic product, such as a bouquet of flowers, customers may focus much less on specific attributes and instead attend to and process information on a global, or holistic, basis.

Comparing and Evaluating Alternatives

Customers seemingly have limited capacities to evaluate and process information. They therefore tend to limit the number of competing products they consider by engaging in simplifying strategies that make choices easier. One of the simplest strategies is called **affect referral**. In this strategy customers do not even bother to examine specific attributes of the product but instead use an evaluation they recall from the past.

In another simple strategy, the **lexicographic heuristic rule**, people first decide which attributes are the most important. Assume that for outboard motors the customer gives fuel efficiency highest priority. The brands being considered are then compared on this attribute. The alternative with the highest rating is chosen. If two or more brands perform equally well on this attribute, the customer will then choose the second most important attribute, perhaps ease of repair, and repeat the process.

The **elimination by aspects model** is another heuristic strategy. As in the lexicographic rule, the customer decides which attribute has the highest priority. Alternative brands are then compared on this attribute, and the alternative that performs most poorly on this attribute is eliminated. Then the customer selects a second important attribute and again eliminates the brand with the worst score. The process continues until only one or a small set of alternatives is left.

Another simplifying strategy is the **conjunctive strategy**, in which the customer sets up minimum cutoff points for each attribute. For example, the customer might say that a particular brand of soup will be considered only if it has fewer than a certain number of calories and less than a certain amount of salt. Any alternative that does not meet these criteria is dropped. A related heuristic is called the **disjunctive heuristic**. In this strategy, any alternative is accepted into the choice set if it meets only one of the minimum standards. For example, the consumer would take any brand of soup that has either fewer than 200 calories or less than 500 mg of salt.

Finally, customers may use the **linear compensatory model**. Here, the customer assigns a weight to each of the attributes. The weight indicates the importance of the attribute. Each of the attributes is then given a score that indicates how well the brand performs on that attribute. The weights are multiplied by the scores and summed across all attributes to arrive at a total score for each brand. The brand with the highest score is selected. The Fishbein model discussed earlier is an example of a linear compensatory model.

Phased strategies are often used to maximize decision accuracy while minimizing the time and effort required to make a decision. The customer first takes a large number of alternatives and uses such simplifying strategies as the conjunctive, disjunctive, or elimination by aspects model to eliminate some of them. That customer then employs some of the more time-consuming but more accurate strategies, such as the linear compensatory model. Phased strategies are quite common.

An obvious marketing implication from the process of phased decision-making strategies is that marketing managers must use the marketing mix to present products so that they are compared and evaluated most favorably. This involves either guiding customers to use a set of heuristics that lead to a favorable evaluation of the managers' products, or designing products so as to be viewed favorably in accordance with heuristics customers already use.

In a group decision-making context, reducing alternatives and coming to a mutually agreeable choice becomes more difficult. In part, this is due to group members having different criteria for evaluating alternatives. They may think different attributes are important, have different goals in mind for the product, have different budgetary requirements, and have different levels of knowledge about product attributes.

Decision-Making Stages

Customer decision making occurs in stages involving certain cognitive and social processes. The number and labeling of these stages vary according to the manager or researcher. Most typically, there is an initial awareness of a product, followed by the development of further knowledge about it, which leads to the creation of certain beliefs about the product and then the emergence of particular feelings or affect about it, which translates into some intention to buy (or not buy), followed by actual purchase (or refusal) behavior. This is often referred to as a **hierarchy of effects model**.

Such models can be useful if or when one understands that these sequences vary; they are not fixed. For example, when a product is highly involving for a consumer or firm because it is quite risky and the decision is important and not easily reversed, that consumer or firm may engage in extensive problem solving in which beliefs based on careful information gathering are developed first, then feelings about particular options are developed, and then a purchase decision is made. However, some decisions are characterized by low involvement in which a buyer may develop some beliefs, make a purchase (behavior) as a way of learning more, and then develop certain feelings about the product. Or there may be a strong set of feelings developed rather quickly whose origins may not be clear. Afterward, certain beliefs will develop that usually support these feelings, and then certain behaviors occur. These behaviors may be considered impulse buying. They may also be stimulated by the need to experience. They may also occur over longer periods of time for significant decisions. Additionally, behavior first situations may occur—for example, when a person receives a product as a gift or as a free sample, a trial period of use, and so on. After actual product use, the customer may develop certain beliefs and/or particular feelings.

Customer Needs

As noted earlier, people are motivated by external stimuli, such as word-of-mouth communication or a product demonstration, and by internal stimuli, such as physical discomfort, the desire to avoid risk, wanting to belong, and seeking to achieve. If these stimuli are strong enough, people will think about the information presented by the stimulus and perhaps seek more information. After processing this information, a gap or discrepancy may be perceived between an actual and a desired state of being, which is referred to as a **need**. The larger the perceived discrepancy or gap between actual and desired states, the greater the need. The greater the need, the greater the tendency to engage in decision processes that will result in choices and their implementation.

The perceived gap between a current state and a feasible desired state is also referred to as a **performance gap**. (The term *need* has many different meanings, and so people often prefer the term *performance gap*.) A performance gap may widen or narrow as perceptions change about the adequacy of the current or actual state or as perceptions change about what is a feasible desired state. A performance gap may arise from (1) the perception of there being a better performing alternative, (2) a perception that the current product or service is no longer performing satisfactorily, or (3) some combination of these perceptions. The two perceptions may interact. Knowing how a new service is superior may cause customers to focus disproportionately more on the corresponding attributes of their current service, thereby becoming more aware of its relative limitations and lowering satisfaction levels with this service.

For example, the speed of a copying machine previously considered by office personnel as fast might now be considered quite slow if its usage increases significantly and people must wait longer to access it. This waiting may produce a desire for a faster machine. However, so long as a replacement is not perceived as feasible (a faster machine isn't available within budget), the performance gap may not become significant. Essentially, users may be resigned to the current situation, but it might eventually produce such adverse consequences that resources will be reallocated from other areas to acquire a new machine. Alternatively, a much faster copying machine may become available under acceptable purchase or leasing terms, potentially fueling a perception of a large performance gap. The wider gap may then activate various decision processes leading to a purchase or lease outcome, if the performance gap is perceived as having an adverse effect for the customer. Much decision making, especially joint decision making, often focuses on defining just how bad the performance gap or need is—that is, how serious the consequences are of not lessening the gap.

Many new goods and services are unsuccessful or less successful than they could be because a firm fails to understand (1) customer perceptions of current states; (2) customer perceptions of desired, feasible states; and (3) what influences these perceptions. Likewise, opportunities for success are often missed because firms fail to understand what activates or influences customers—that is, what arouses, channels, and sustains customer behavior, particularly when latent or emerging needs are involved.

Managers sometimes claim that no one can understand consumer needs, particularly before having a product or service to offer, because people don't always know what they need or want; or if they do, they can't express their needs adequately, or they don't know what they need because they don't know what is and isn't possible for addressing a problem. Indeed, at any given time, the vast majority of human mental and physical states are not at a level of awareness. People simply couldn't function if they were always conscious of even most of their thoughts, knowledge, feelings, emotions, and physiological requirements and the brain evolved with this consideration in mind.

Additionally, communicating needs and explaining the "why" of behavior can be difficult, and certainly consumers cannot be aware of everything that is technically feasible to satisfy a need even if they understood their needs and behaviors exactly and with full awareness. Thus, the task of understanding important customer needs can be very challenging and the ultimate knowledge gained often incomplete. Were it otherwise, everyone would be doing it effectively, and there would be little competitive advantage to the firm that (1) attempts to understand customers and (2) uses this understanding creatively.

The willingness to seek understanding and use incomplete information imaginatively is one of the distinguishing characteristics of particularly successful managers. The difficulties many managers have, especially those in nonmarketing functions, in understanding customer needs are usually rooted in the failure to grasp that:

- Needs have no meaning on their own but must be understood within certain contexts.

- One must think in terms of clusters of needs.

- Needs have sociological, psychological, and physiological origins or determinants to be understood.

- Innovative research technologies are available to understand the meaning, clustering, and determinants of needs.

Fortunately, the state of the art with respect to customer research coupled with the right decision-making process permits managers to learn a great deal that can be helpful in identifying need-based opportunities and in designing better goods and services. This occurs by a process of successive approximation. By using appropriate thinking tools and formal market research, and by carefully examining their own personal experience, managers can formulate initial ideas, obtain feedback, develop more specific ideas, obtain additional feedback, refine ideas still further, and so on. Thus managers can proceed from exploratory thinking, to developmental thinking, to confirmatory evaluations using experience and formal methods of market research together.

Market research methods may range from ethnographic research, to surveys, to the use of mathematical models and simulations. When planned well, this evolutionary process can be done on a very timely basis and be quite effective and efficient in understanding latent needs, developing appropriate goods and services, and creating strategies for promoting and delivering them.

Although not discussed here, research techniques are available that enable customers to express thoughts and feelings that are often hidden but that accurately represent and describe their motivations and needs. Moreover, researchers can find important underlying factors widely shared among particular customer segments or groups. Techniques are available that enable managers to identify the relative importance of these factors under different conditions and for different types of people. Thus, very useful insights can be developed in a timely way about what, when, why, and for whom something is important. The "something" may be basic motivation, values, product attributes, product functions, brand image, consumption situations, purchase settings, or, typically, a combination of "somethings."

Using still other techniques, further customer feedback can be obtained that, when used imaginatively, can result in a more specific response—say, a prototype of a new product. Customer reactions to the prototype may yield changes that permit a still more refined response to customer needs. And the process continues to test marketing and later to product modifications after full-scale launch.

Throughout the entire process of learning about and responding to customer needs, managers must use both their accumulated wisdom as well as formal research. A manager's accumulated knowledge and special perspective make research or information applicable, but that manager must critically examine and not blindly accept this accumulated wisdom and formal research.

Social Systems

One of the most intriguing and important patterns of human behavior is the tendency of people to differentiate themselves from one another and yet to group together on the basis of important similarities. This behavior is central to marketing strategy, particularly strategies involving market segments. Market segments are subsets of customers who are homogeneous with respect to key thinking, behaviors, and other characteristics. People or organizations in one subset share important similarities that also differentiate them from other subsets or segments. Goods and services are then developed, distributed, and promoted in ways that are consistent with these patterns.

There are countless ways of segmenting markets. One way is on the basis of geopolitical boundaries consisting of countries as well as regions among and even within countries. These are macro social systems. People in each such large-scale system will share common patterns of thinking and behaving. In a very general way, these common patterns are referred to as **culture**. A **subculture** is a division of a larger culture based on some characteristic, such as social status or ethnicity, that produces similar behaviors that distinguish the group from the larger culture. These are micro, or small-scale, social systems.

An important type of social system consists of a chain of customers in a distribution channel. For instance, in many industrial settings a manufacturer may sell to another manufacturer, who sells to an independent distributor, who, in turn, has its own customers, and so on. The greater the understanding each vendor in this chain has of its customers' customers, the more opportunity it has to create value in its products. This encourages long-term partnerships that foster the development of goods and services that help one's customers to be more effective in their markets. Even in ultimate consumer settings, the resale and trade-in value of a product may be an important criterion in the purchase decision process.

A major challenge for managers is to determine what cultural (and subcultural) differences are important and how to respond to such differences. The failure to differentiate products and communications on the basis of cultural differences can be very costly. Likewise, making unnecessary changes in the marketing mix for different market segments may also be very costly. So an important issue is, when are cultural differences sufficient or insufficient enough to warrant changes in marketing practice? Like so many issues, it is important because there are no easy answers.

Universals

People who study cultures tend to highlight differences between cultures or subcultures, and for a good reason: culture explains a considerable part of all behavior. However, recent thinking among anthropologists is also giving more attention to what are called **human universals** or **near universals**. These are traits and behaviors that are found in very nearly all societies. This focus has been stimulated in part by findings that have overturned widely held previous beliefs about the distinctiveness of different cultures. For example, Margaret Mead argued that adolescence in Samoa did not involve the same trauma as found in Western societies; Bronislaw Malinowski argued that the Oedipus complex was peculiar only to certain types of societies; Edward Sapir and Benjamin Whorf hypothesized that categories of language shape perceptions of the world; and others have argued that the meaning of facial expression varies by culture. These important and influential beliefs have all been found to be in error. For example, the evidence is much more supportive of the idea that thought shapes language rather than the reverse. Where differences in thinking exist among people who speak different languages, they are not found to be the result of qualities inherent in those people's spoken or written language, although such differences are important in other ways.

A small sample of universal or near universal qualities is presented in figure 2-4 to provide the reader with a flavor of what these are. Literally hundreds of other such qualities have been identified. Fortunately, the list of universals that are relevant for a product category or for a specific brand concept and positioning is relatively brief. Some managers and researchers recommend identifying the relevant universals prior to introducing a product into a new cultural market. The universals represent either a specific need or the source of a specific need to which a product should be linked. Then these managers and researchers ask whether in each market these universals manifest themselves in different ways that might require changes in the marketing mix. This often involves learning what metaphors customers use or find meaningful to express these themes.

Monitoring changes in the way universals are enacted also provides a basis for determining whether changes in the marketing mix are necessary. It also provides a basis for identifying opportunities for new goods and services. For instance, if people in two different market segments are becoming more similar or less similar in how they conceive of success and failure, then some standardization in communications might be appropriate or inappropriate for products related to the achievement of success and avoidance of failure. If issues of success and failure are becoming more salient in a particular culture, then this might represent an opportunity for a new product or a new concept for an existing product. Knowing, for example, that fashion and food products—that is, what people place on and in their bodies—relate to a widely held need

FIGURE 2-4

Universals

• Use metaphors • Have a system of status and roles • Divide labor by sex and age • Share cognitive organization • Regulate the expression of affect • Use space • Record numbers • Create art and artistic activities • Conceive of success and failure • Have standards by which beauty and ugliness are measured • Are ethnocentric • Choose pragmatically • Have followers of leaders who are apathetic, regimented, "mature," and autarkic • Believe in the supernatural • Have a range of temperaments • Categorize color • Empathize • Dominate • Imagine • Personify • Create solitary groups antagonistic to outsiders • Imitate outside influences • Resist outside influences • Compete individually and in groups • Hold similar attitudes toward supernatural occurrences, fear, hope, love, hate, good, bad, beauty, ugliness, murder, theft, lying, and rape • Dance • Sing • Tell tales • Create literary art • Use figurative language • Create verse that uses beats and lines • Change the language over time • Symbolize • Establish rules and leadership to govern the allocation of important resources • Trade and transport goods • Conduct activities by dyads and groups • Adjust joint activities to personalities • Establish rules and regulations • Develop similar cognitive functions • Consider some aspects of sexuality private • Adorn ourselves • Practice abortion • Think about social relations between other individuals: triangular awareness • Associate art with ritual • Establish etiquette • Need novelty • Use words denoting motion, giving, corporeal objects, kin, dimension, color, value, human propensity, physical property, and speed • Experience approach-avoid ambivalence • Are curious • Express emotion with our faces • Interpret rather than merely observe human behavior • Transform and elaborate the human body • Envy • Use symbolic means to cope with envy • Exchange • Settle disputes • Reciprocate (in both positive and negative [tit-for-tat] ways) • Give gifts • Use logic and the logical notions of relationship • Orient in space and time • Are motivated • Recognize property rights • Associate music with ritual • Are consciously aware of memory, emotions, experience of acting in the world and making decisions • Distinguish between public and private • Experience being in control as opposed to under control • Decide collectively • Have organizations distinct from the family • Follow rules about inheritance • Experience dyadic conflict • Display personality apart from social role • Recognize ascribed vs. achieved status • Deny unwelcome facts • Use mood-altering drugs • Prefer faces that are average in their dimensions • Perform hairdressing rituals • Give hair symbolic value • Use language with a universal underlying structure • Overestimate the objectivity of our thought • Expect parental care and training of children • Provide for the poor and unfortunate • Recognize economic obligations in relationship to exchanges of goods and services • Demand truth in certain conditions • Are unable to transcend guilt • Are aggressive • Hope • Forget • Get anxious • Appreciate aesthetics • Create solidarity • Need privacy and silence occasionally • Need to explain the world • Sacrifice ourselves for our group • Consume substances to partake of their properties • Think men and women are different in more than only procreative ways • Lie • Use and understand the concept of equity and most of the West's other general legal concepts • Celebrate special occasions when people try to look their best • Wish to allure • Desire to stand out from others • Feel pride, shame, amusement, and shock • Forgo present pleasure for a deferred good • Use the same basic color categories • Identify the same geometric forms • Consider the relationship of nature to culture • Look at our way of life against others • Consider morally right and wrong methods of satisfying needs • Form a personality structure that integrates needs (id), values (superego), and executive-response processes (ego) • Attach meaning to what is essentially meaningless

Source: Adapted from D. E. Brown, *Human Universals* (New York: McGraw-Hill, 1991), 157–201.

of self-expression may help in developing a common promotional theme to be used for these products in several countries.[4] Moreover, there may be certain visual cues, such as a discotheque or soccer game, that have the same or similar meaning in several countries and that will activate ideas about self-expression that are relevant to the food or fashion product being advertised. This can result in a more efficient use of promotional and packaging resources.

Distinctions

While there are important universals among all societies, they are often expressed or manifested in very different ways. This means that while a product or service may address a need or cluster of needs shared by many different markets, it may have to be designed, delivered, and communicated in very different ways corresponding to how different customers think and behave with respect to that need.

Moreover, when thinking about international markets, the country may not be the appropriate unit of analysis. For a certain target market such as young adults in several countries, fashion ads that use lifestyle formats, fantasy, visuals, emotions, and self-identity may have more universal appeal than ads for the same product whose execution gives more attention to culture, art, history, and more abstract concepts. The latter themes will appeal more to older adults in these countries. In this case, differences exist not so much across or between countries as between segments or subcultures related to chronological age.

The idea that the marketing mix can be standardized across international boundaries is often debated. It is an attractive idea because of the potential cost savings and the fact that in some ways (and for various reasons) people in different social systems are becoming more similar. However, the evidence suggests that (1) successful standardization is the exception, not the rule; (2) some important differentiation is often required, particularly in advertising; and (3) firms that fail to explicitly consider differentiating their marketing mix (independently of the conclusion reached) are likely to fail or be much less successful than would otherwise be the case.

Consider the simple strawberry fruit.[5] Nearly all people in all societies have an explicit need for healthy food products and a simultaneous need to indulge in the pleasures of foods that happen to be less healthy. This example is a special cluster of seemingly contradictory needs. It was determined in food tests in four countries that when a strawberry was added to a picture of a slice of cake, the cake took on an even greater appearance of indulgence, decadence, and sweetness. The cake was perceived as less appealing as a special dessert when the strawberry was absent. At the same time, in all four countries, when strawberries were added to a bowl of breakfast cereal, the cereal was perceived by the same people as being more healthy and natural than when the strawberry was absent. The same pictures were used as stimuli in all four countries.

This finding alone might have led an organization concerned with the promotion of strawberries or of cake and cereal products to present strawberries in all advertising of these products in each country. Fortunately, in-depth interviews were conducted with customers participating in the tests to learn why the same fruit could add a sense of both decadence and health depending on the context. Clues were uncovered and then explored in further testing in which it was learned, for example, that in country A the strawberries on the cake should be sliced, while they should remain whole when presented in the cereal, and that in country B the reverse should be done. It was also determined, once it was understood why the strawberry could be effective with both food products, that in two of the countries there were other fruits that had an even stronger impact. Thus different advertising was developed for each country involving different fruits and/or different ways of presenting the fruit to make the food products more appealing.

In that example, initial testing implied that a standardized advertising approach would be warranted. But deeper analyses of customer thinking suggested that differentiated promotional strategies in each country would be significantly more effective than standardized advertising would be. This conclusion was confirmed by additional follow-up research.

These deeper insights will be increasingly important as the primary source of competitive advantage in the future. Deeper insights are important because they are likely to be shared by otherwise diverse consumers, and they are more durable or less likely to change. They also permit more creative use by managers.

Summary

This chapter reviewed the following themes: marketing's customer focus, the importance of understanding the customer, unit of analysis, modeling customer behavior, forming attitudes, comparing and evaluating alternatives, decision-making stages, customer needs, and social systems. In every marketing situation, which is to say, whenever exchanges occur, using ideas such as these to understand the customer's perspective is a critical first step in the analysis that will ultimately lead to more effective marketing decisions. Thus, beyond knowing that many concepts and tools are available to help them understand, predict, and influence customers, managers must develop the habit of mind in which these concepts and tools are used regularly and with imagination to understand the voice of the customer.

Additional Resources for Gaining Consumer Insights

Koiso-Kanttila, Nina. "Time, Attention, Authenticity and Consumer Benefits of the Web." *Business Horizons*, January 15, 2005. This article addresses three potential consumer behavior tendencies: perceived time scarcity, competition for consumers' attention, and quest for authenticity.

Loveman, Gary W. "Diamonds in the Data Mine." *Harvard Business Review*, May 2003. Harrah's Entertainment CEO and former Harvard Business School professor Gary Loveman explains how his company has trumped its competitors by mining customer data, running experiments using customer information, and using the findings to implement marketing strategies that keep customers coming back for more.

Zaltman, Gerald. "Hidden Minds." *Harvard Business Review*, June 2002. Harvard Business School professor emeritus Gerald Zaltman discusses his novel market-research method for revealing consumers' unconscious thoughts about everything from fabric sprays to the Internet.

Zaltman, Gerald. *How Customers Think: Essential Insights into the Mind of the Market*. Boston: Harvard Business School Press, 2003.

Notes

1. Additional Resources were added to this chapter. They did not appear in the Class Note. The following references appeared as footnotes in the Class Note.

2. There are literally dozens of textbooks and journals devoted to the topic of customer behavior and several professional associations concerned with the topic.

3. M. Fishbein and I. Ajzen, *Belief, Attitude, Intention, and Behavior: An Introduction to Theory and Research* (Reading, MA: Addison-Wesley, 1975), 389–400 as quoted in Park and Zaltman.

4. T. J. Domzal and J. B. Kernan, "Mirror, Mirror: Some Postmodern Reflections on Global Advertising," *Journal of Advertising* 22 (1993).

5. This example is somewhat disguised and simplified.

Part II

Developing Marketing Strategies

3.

Market Segmentation, Target Market Selection, and Positioning

AFTER THE MARKETING ANALYSIS PHASE, THE NEXT stage in the marketing process consists of the following three steps:

1. Market segmentation

2. Target market selection

3. Product positioning

These steps are the prerequisites for designing a successful marketing strategy. They allow the firm to focus its efforts on the right

This chapter was written by Miklos Sarvary and Anita Elberse and originally published as "Market Segmentation, Target Market Selection, and Positioning," Class Note 9-506-019 (Boston: Harvard Business School Publishing, 2005), a revised version of a note by M. Sarvary. It was lightly edited for consistency.

customers and also provide the organizing force for the marketing mix elements. Product positioning, in particular, provides the synergy among the four *P*s (product, price, place, and promotion) of the marketing plan.[1]

This chapter elaborates on each of the three steps.

Market Segmentation

Market segmentation consists of dividing the market into groups of (potential) customers—called "market segments"—with distinct characteristics, behaviors, or needs. The aim is to cluster customers in groups that clearly differ from each other but show a great deal of homogeneity within the group. As such, compared with a large, heterogeneous market, those segments can be served more efficiently and effectively with products that match their needs.

It is important that the segments are sufficiently different from each other. In addition, it is critical that the segmentation is based on one or more customer characteristics that are relevant to the firm's marketing effort. A thorough analysis of the customers is essential in that regard. There are two (related) types of segmentation:

1. Segmentation based on benefits sought by customers

2. Segmentation based on observable characteristics of customers

In an ideal scenario, marketers will typically want to segment customers based on the benefits they seek from a particular product. That is, they will try to group customers based on their needs. Take the example of nonprescription drugs treating pain, inflammation, and fever. Market research has revealed that people evaluate these drugs along two dimensions: effectiveness and gentleness. There are two basic segments, each valuing one of these dimensions more than the other. Thus, there is one segment that prefers an effective drug even if it has side effects, while the other segment prefers a less effective drug provided that it is gentler—that is, without side effects. The two segments represent benefit segments in that they are based on differences in consumers' preferences or needs.

In practice, marketers tend to delineate segments based on some observable characteristics. Most often, marketers use consumer demographics (such as gender, age, and income), consumers' geographic location, their lifestyles, or behavioral characteristics (such as usage occasions) to create segments. The motivation is clear. Segments created in such a way are easy to identify and address with a marketing message. It is important to realize, however, that such segmentation only works to the extent that it is correlated with benefit segments. In the previous example about nonprescription painkillers, it happens to be the case that older people tend to belong to the benefit segment that values the drugs' gentleness while younger consumers prefer potent drugs even if they have side effects. Age, therefore, is a good variable to segment the market in this case. Age groups are easy to target, and, in this case, age strongly correlates with distinct consumer preferences.

In summary, segmentation requires the following steps from the marketer:

- Understand the benefits that customers seek

- Segment the market and develop prototypical customer profiles based on the customer benefits

- Find the observable variables (such as demographic characteristics) that are most likely to discriminate between the benefit segments to identify membership in specific segments

The segmentation process may seem quite straightforward, but in practice it requires quite a bit of experience and creativity. One complicating factor is that there can be multiple acceptable benefit segmentation schemes. In general, a satisfactory, actionable market segmentation typically requires multiple iterations and informed compromises from the marketer.

Target Market Selection

Target market selection involves evaluating each market segment's attractiveness and selecting one or more of the market segments to enter. It is the next logical step following segmentation. Once the firm understands the structure of consumer demand, it has to decide which segments it wants to serve and how. In addition to a solid understanding of the customer, analyses of the competitive environment and the company are instrumental to the task of target market selection. The objective is to select segments in such a way that the firm maximizes its profit.

In the case of over-the-counter painkillers discussed earlier, there are two basic types of drugs competing on the market. One is based on aspirin (e.g., Bayer), and the other is based on acetaminophen (e.g., Tylenol). It turns out that aspirin is more effective but has side effects causing minor stomach irritation. Thus, it is natural for firms producing these different drugs to focus on the segments that best fit their products. In this case, target market selection is relatively simple. In other cases, more elaborate analyses may be required to choose the appropriate segments to serve.

The key to target market selection is understanding differentiation. It involves collecting and comparing data on the company and its competitors to evaluate who is most likely to succeed serving each of the identified segments. The process starts by collecting data for each firm in five areas:

1. Ability to conceive and design

2. Ability to produce (quality and quantity)

3. Ability to market

4. Ability to finance

5. Ability to manage/execute

Each of these five general areas can be divided into more concrete items. For example, in the "ability to conceive and design" category, the marketer may want to evaluate competitors' R&D capability (as reflected in the size and experience of the design group as well as the R&D budget), existing patents and copyrights, access to new technologies through third parties, and so on. Similarly, to assess a firm's "ability to produce," competitors' production technology and capacity as well as flexibility may need to be evaluated.

Once the necessary data are collected, they can be synthesized into so-called competitor capability matrices. One matrix is needed for each segment. In each matrix, the detailed items of the evaluation areas are listed in the rows, and the relevant firms—including both the firm itself and its competitors—are listed in the columns. Each entry consists of a rating (say, on a ten-point scale) of the competitor on the item corresponding to the entry. This format allows the marketer to recognize patterns in the competitive environment and identify the segment (or segments) where the marketer's firm is likely to be the strongest player. If there are too many items in the rows (as is often the case), it is useful to replicate the matrix by listing only those items that represent critical success factors in the product category. This enables a more parsimonious evaluation of the situation.

It is important to recognize that this differential advantage analysis facilitates target market selection by pointing out the relative strengths (and weaknesses) of the focal firm, but this analysis does not predict the competitive reactions the firm might face if the firm indeed decides to target a segment. Anticipating such reactions typically requires a careful analysis of competitors' overall corporate strategies and their reputation or history for competitive behavior.

Positioning

The chapter "Marketing Strategy" defined *positioning* as the marketer's effort to identify a unique selling proposition for the product. It is arranging for a product to occupy a clear, distinctive, and attractive position relative to competing products in the minds of target consumers.

A good positioning statement answers three questions:

1. Who are the customers?

2. What is the set of needs that the product fulfills?

3. Why is the product the best option to satisfy those needs?

In finding a desirable positioning, the firm has to consider, for each potential segment, how it would approach serving that group of customers, and how it would want to be perceived by those customers. The answers should be based on a thorough understanding of the customer, the competitive environment, the company itself, and the conditions of the market in which the company operates.

The Positioning Statement

It is typically helpful to formalize the considerations in a positioning statement that specifies the place the firm wishes to occupy in its target customers' minds. One commonly used form is shown in figure 3-1.

The positioning statement is primarily directed to potential customers. This statement has a guiding role in the development of the marketing plan—marketing practitioners often say that "solving" the positioning problem enables a company to solve its marketing mix problem. For example, if a computer company finds that a market segment with budgetary constraints prefers its products because they are significantly cheaper than competitive offerings, it

FIGURE 3-1

Fill-in-the-blank positioning statement

Our product/brand	is	(single most important claim)
among all		(competitive frame)
because		(single most important support)

could aim for a no-frills product line, closely monitor its price advantage, emphasize the low price in its advertising, and employ a direct-to-consumer channel strategy that limits the markup on its products. Similarly, if a sports apparel firm understands that customers in its desired market segment buy products that make them feel like professional athletes, it could seek such endorsements from top-ranking athletes and use that in its advertising; emphasize innovative, top-of-the-line products; primarily use a high-end sports retailing channel; and aim for a higher price point.

A firm's desired positioning thus is the organizing force between the marketing mix elements to ensure synergy among them. It is also important for internal communication within the firm. It provides the identity to the firm. For example, IBM's famous claim "The solution to your problem is IBM" helped change the firm's internal culture by teaching employees to be problem solvers for their customers.

Differentiation

As that statement from IBM indicates, a good positioning reflects a competitive differentiation. A positioning statement should go beyond clearly articulating to customers the benefits that the product fulfills—it should also be clearly differentiated from competitive offerings. A firm will not want to introduce products targeted at needs that are already sufficiently served by competitors, as it could lead to an intense price competition and leave no profit to the firm. Consider the two extreme types of differentiation:

1. If all buyers agree that product A is better than product B, they are **vertically differentiated**. Consequently, if product A and B are sold at the same price, nobody will buy product B.

2. If products A and B differ in ways independent of buyers' overall judgments about the products' quality levels, those products are **horizontally differentiated**. If A and B are sold at the same price, some people will prefer one, some another.

A positioning strategy based on a horizontal differentiation makes use of the fact that consumers differ in their tastes. For example, in the category of passenger cars, some consumers like small cars and others like minivans, while still others like SUVs. Each of these groups consists of a relatively homogeneous set of people with similar needs. A firm pursuing a horizontal differentiation strategy should identify the group(s) whose need(s) are not sufficiently served by a competitor.

Vertical differentiation also exploits the fact that consumers are different but takes advantage of consumers' differences in their willingness to pay for quality. In a pure vertically differentiated world, all customers (and potential customers) agree on the relevant dimensions of product quality. In the example of passenger cars, quality can be a combination of speed, comfort, and reliability. In addition, all customers prefer more quality to less. However, they differ in their valuation of quality. Staying with the example of passenger cars, most consumers prefer a BMW to a Ford, but only few can—or would be willing to—pay the price for the BMW. A firm pursuing a vertical differentiation strategy should position products to customers with a specific level of willingness to pay for quality that is not sufficiently served by a competitor.

In practice, in most product categories, marketers have the option to differentiate their products both horizontally and vertically. Creativity and marketing expertise plays an important role. Some skilled marketers may discover or "create" a set of needs among customers that are not yet served, or tap into a market segment that was previously not regarded as a viable group of customers to serve. Some firms even completely change the paradigm of differentiation in a category—for example, by moving the focus from performance to style, as in Swatch's redefinition of the watches category.

All elements of the marketing mix can be the primary instrument of differentiation. Product attributes or features are often a key differentiator (think of the importance of packaging for environmentally conscious or "green" consumers, for example). Price can be a useful signal of quality and thus a tool for vertical differentiation. Place can bring critical advantages (examples are online distribution, where consumers can shop in the privacy of their own home, or vending machines, where products are available instantaneously and twenty-four hours a day). Promotion is an obvious tool to communicate to consumers to what extent and along what dimensions the product is different from other alternatives.

The Role of Brands

Positioning and branding are inextricably linked. Brands can be thought of simply as nouns that marketers have introduced into consumers' language to make product differentiation concrete. At a minimum, these marketers want to assert that their offering is not like those of their competitors. When marketers call a fruit juice "Snapple," for instance, they are asserting that it is worth noting some special distinctions between Snapple and all other fruit juices. Some of these assertions can be viewed as promises or pledges about attributes of the product. Other assertions may have to do with how Snapple users are differentiated from cola users, or how Snapple usage occasions are differentiated from other beverage usage occasions. Most ambitiously, a brand can assert that it is the category. Perhaps the highest goal to which brand builders can aspire is to have the noun that they have imposed on the language displace the natural-language word (as in using "Kleenex" to denote facial tissue, or speaking of "Fedexing" a package or "Xeroxing" a document). However, not all brands come to mean what the marketers have intended, and many brands struggle to denote anything that the consumer finds worthy of notice.

Summary

This chapter covers three steps—customer segmentation, target market selection, and positioning—that contribute to the design of a successful marketing strategy. These steps focus a company's marketing efforts on the right customers and organize the elements of the marketing mix. The discussion of brands—specifically brand development, differentiation, and valuation—continues in the chapters titled "Marketing Communications and Promotions" and "Product Policy."

Additional Readings on Segmentation, Positioning, and Differentiation

Beverland, Michael, and Michael Ewing. "Slowing the Adoption and Diffusion Process to Enhance Brand Repositioning: The Consumer Driven Repositioning of Dunlop Volley." *Business Horizons*, September 15, 2005. The authors explore how to create long-term brand value by rejecting hard-sell marketing, targeting alternative distribution channels, and delaying launch to the mainstream audience.

Deighton, John. "How Snapple Got Its Juice Back." *Harvard Business Review*, January 2002. There is a vital interplay between a brand's challenges and the culture of its owner. This article discusses why Quaker's textbook marketing approach backfired, whereas Triarc's revival of Snapple's original anything-goes attitude worked.

Kim, W. Chan, and Renée Mauborgne. "Blue Ocean Strategy: From Theory to Practice." *California Management Review*, April 1, 2005. The authors present a set of analytical tools and frameworks that can enable firms to develop uncontested markets for their products and services.[2]

Levitt, Theodore. "Marketing Success Through Differentiation—of Anything," *Harvard Business Review*, January 1980. In this classic article, the author explains how marketers can differentiate any product or service, even commodities that seem to differ only in price from competitors' offerings.

Yankelovich, Daniel, and David Meer. "Rediscovering Market Segmentation." *Harvard Business Review*, February 2006. The authors describe the elements of a smart segmentation strategy and introduce their "gravity of decision spectrum," a tool that gauges the importance that consumers place on a product.

Notes

1. Summary, Additional Readings, and Notes were added to this chapter. They did not appear in the Class Note.

2. For in-depth coverage, see W. C. Kim and R. Mauborgne's *Blue Ocean Strategy* (Boston: Harvard Business School Press, 2005).

4.

Product Policy

FIRMS FACE A WIDE VARIETY OF CRITICAL PRODUCT policy decisions.[1] Some examples of issues that frequently emerge are:

- What product attributes or features should be offered? What is the preferred trade-off between the costs made to develop a product and the customer value delivered?

- How should a firm respond when, some time after a successful product launch, competitors are catching up with "me-too" products?

- How should a firm structure its new product development pipeline?

- What is the preferred composition of the product mix? When is it time to extend the product line or brand and

This chapter was written by Anita Elberse and originally published as "Principles of Product Policy," Class Note 9-506-018 (Boston: Harvard Business School Publishing, 2005). She based part of the material on an earlier note, R. J. Dolan, "Product Policy Decisions," Class Note 9-501-049 (Boston: Harvard Business School Publishing, 2000). It was lightly edited for consistency.

with what type of extension? How can the firm avoid dilut-
ing the brand?

- When should a firm prune the product offerings? When is it
  time to trade down the product line by offering a cheaper
  version of an existing product?

This chapter attempts to shed light on the key issues related to
the product *P* of the marketing mix (price, place, and promotion
are the three other *P*s).

Products, Product Mixes, and Product Extensions

Products

A product can be defined as anything that is offered to a market
for consumption (in one form or another) and that satisfies a need.
Products can be classified along a number of dimensions, including:

- The nature of customers' buying behavior: Marketers typically
  speak of convenience goods when products are frequently
  purchased without much deliberation. Such goods are typically widely available. The purchase of shopping goods involves more planning and some comparison shopping by
  customers. Specialty goods are characterized by relatively in-
  elastic demand and little or no comparison shopping. They
  are only available in selected outlets.

- The level of involvement in the purchase process: A related
  dimension, products are often characterized as either **low
  involvement**, meaning requiring little deliberation by customers, or **high involvement**, meaning that customers
  invest significant time and effort in the purchase process.

- The type of benefit: Some products deliver mostly **functional**
  or utilitarian benefits (i.e., have a logical, rational advan-

tage), while other products primarily address an **emotional**, ego-expressive need.

While it is often helpful to think of these product classes, it is important to recognize that different customers may place the same products in entirely different classes. Similarly, different manufacturers competing in the same product category may position their products at opposite sides of the spectrum.

Products can be divided into **tangible goods** (i.e., physical products) and **intangible goods** (such as services, events, people, places, and ideas). Services are offerings that do not result in the ownership of anything—think of hotels, legal services, or consulting. However, in practice, many products have both a tangible and an intangible component. Examples are everywhere: coffee shops sell coffee in a comfortable atmosphere and often allow customers to stick around as long as they want, car dealers usually sell cars with the promise of free checkups and discounted repair services, and restaurants often offer to box leftovers.

These examples illustrate that products are often bundles of benefits that satisfy customer needs. As depicted in figure 4-1, marketers distinguish the core product and the augmented product.

FIGURE 4-1

Core and augmented product

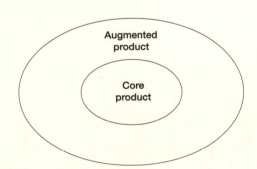

Source: T. Levitt, "Marketing Success Through Differentiation—of Anything," *Harvard Business Review*, January–February 1980.

The **core product** is what consumers are actually buying—it serves a direct, primary benefit. The **augmented product** offers additional benefits. Consider the example of Snapple's grape juice. When consumers buy this product, the core product they are buying is juice packaged in a bottle with a colored label. It can serve to quench thirst. However, for many consumers, there are other benefits: buying Snapple juice may give them a sense they are treating themselves to something special, for example, or make them feel they belong to a group of people with a quirky, off-beat lifestyle. For customers who appreciate these added benefits, the augmented product is more valuable than the core product—they are willing to pay more for grape juice in a Snapple bottle than for the same blend in a generic bottle, even if it comes from the same grapes.

In the Snapple example, brand associations enhance the core product. As also indicated in the chapter titled "Market Segmentation, Target Market Selection, and Positioning," brands are a crucial aspect of most product offerings. **Brands** are names or symbols that marketers have introduced to make product differentiation concrete. They assert that a firm's products are different from those offered by competitors. **Brand equity** is the term used for the positive effect that the brand has on a potential customer of a product—it reflects how much more consumers are willing to pay for a particular brand compared with a competing brand (or with a generic product).

However, augmentation can come in a variety of ways. Other important tools of differentiation are customer service, installation, repair and delivery services, warranties, and credit possibilities. As products mature and competitors are introducing "me-too" products that efficiently deliver the same core product attributes, firms can use such augmentations to create a sustainable differentiated offering. Intangibles like brands and services are often particularly helpful differentiation tools because they are relatively hard to copy by competitors. Because of the relatively high costs associated with building brands or offering quality customer service, and because of the uncertain pay-off of such investments, competitors are often reluctant to match those expenses in the short run.

In sum, when making product policy decisions, marketers must:

- Recognize the core customer need they intend to satisfy

- Verify whether their core product is ideally suited to satisfy that need and, if not, how it can be redesigned

- Understand how they can best augment their core product to create the bundle of benefits that will provide the most satisfying customer experience and shield the company from threats by competitors

Product Mixes

It is typically useful to consider critical product policy decisions in the context of a firm's product mix. A **product mix** encompasses all product lines. A **product line** is a group of items that serve a similar function. For example, Snapple's product mix is made up of five product lines: iced tea, lemonade, juice, water, and Snapple-On-Ice popsicles.[2]

Each product line can be described in terms of its *length*, which refers to the number of items within the product line (e.g., Lemon, Lime Green, Raspberry, and Peach iced tea flavors), and *depth*, which refers to the number of versions of each product in the line (e.g., Lemon and Diet Lemon). Each firm faces the task of determining the optimal product line length and depth, as well as the optimal number of product lines.

It is often also useful to consider the *consistency* of a product mix (i.e., the extent to which the product lines share relevant characteristics)—for example, that they draw on the same underlying technology or serve the same market segment. Since four or five Snapple product lines are beverages that are consumed in similar ways and, presumably, by similar consumer segments, and its line of popsicles may largely appeal to the same segment, most marketers would describe its product mix as highly consistent.

Product lines can stretch out on horizontal and vertical dimensions. Snapple's offerings differ on a horizontal level in that they do not differ in an objective sense—it is a matter of consumer taste whether Snapple's cranberry raspberry is better than its Snapple apple or vice versa. In a vertical product line, products are more clearly delineated on a price or performance basis.

Product Line and Brand Extensions

Firms seeking to increase the number of offerings can do so in a number of ways. Figure 4-2 captures four basic options.

As the figure indicates, **line extensions** are existing brands extended to new product forms in an existing product category. For example, if Snapple were to launch a new juice flavor that also bears the Snapple name, it qualifies as a line extension. A **brand extension** is an existing brand extended to new product forms in a new product category. If Snapple decides to move into, say, the beer category or to start a clothing line with the Snapple logo, that would constitute a brand extension. Line extensions are more common than brand extensions.

FIGURE 4-2

New products and brands

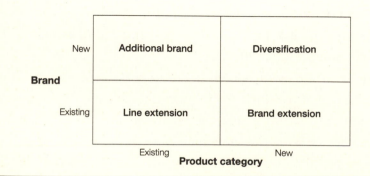

In some instances—for example, when associations that consumers have with a certain brand are thought to hinder the takeoff of a new product—firms launch new products under a new brand. When the firm adds an additional brand in an existing category, it engages in a **multibrand strategy**. When it does so in a new product category, it seeks diversification in its products and brands. Given the costs usually associated with establishing new brands, such decisions must be considered carefully.

New Product Development

The development of new products, ranging from product modifications to truly original products, is a critical activity for firms seeking to remain profitable in the long term. New product development typically encompasses a number of general stages, such as:

- Idea generation and screening

- Concept development and testing

- Physical product development and testing

- Commercialization

The exact nature of the development process greatly differs across industries, products, and firms. For example, in the pharmaceutical industry, the development of a new drug often starts with thousands of compounds, of which, after years of extensive clinical trials, perhaps only one may turn out to be an effective and commercially viable drug. In the music industry, on the other hand, one bout of inspiration could be sufficient to generate a hit song in as little as a few hours. Sometimes, the development process starts with a well-articulated customer need (such as the necessity to have a cure for a particular ailment), while at other times, the need addressed by an innovation only becomes apparent after customers are exposed to it.

Some products are breakthroughs in that they establish a new product category (Sony's Walkman is a legendary example), but the majority of new products are entries into an established product category that hope to achieve success by being better than existing competitors—at least in the eyes of some substantial part of the market.

It is vital for firms to have a well-thought-out process behind their product development—and to actually use and constantly adjust that process. Many firms have highly formalized, structured processes that become an impediment rather than stimulus to thinking as managers just go through the motions of the process. Four hallmarks of an effective process are:

1. The voice of the customer is heard throughout the development process: A variety of research techniques, such as customer surveys, can be useful to gain insights into what customers want. However, such research also has its shortcomings—for example, when the firm intends to design a breakthrough product that goes beyond target users' current experience. In those cases, the voice of the customer must be anticipated or sensed. **Empathic design**, wherein users' preferences are sensed through empathy with their situation rather than through explicit inquiry, is often a useful technique in such cases.

2. Substantial work is done before physical production begins, across firms' different functional areas (such as marketing, engineering, and manufacturing): Firms often quickly push products into the design or production stage—for instance, to create a tangible sign that the process is moving quickly. Often, however, this is at the cost of later, expensive redesigns or failures in the marketplace.

3. The process has real go/no-go decision points: A proper new product development process is often described as a "funnel," in which a number of ideas are generated and, in each sub-

sequent development stage, some are rejected while others pass the test and continue on, leading to an ever narrowing number of still serving ideas. However, in reality, firms frequently do not give enough consideration to actually killing product ideas once they have passed an initial, weak test.

4. The process recognizes the firm's distinctive competencies: That is, the process not only assesses the product-market fit but also the product-company fit and the market-company fit, and considers how the firm's capabilities correspond to those of its competitors and collaborators.

The ultimate objective of the new product development process is, of course, to generate a product that delivers superior value to the target customers. It is their perception of value that counts. In new markets, when there is no directly competitive offering, customers will define the value of a new product by comparing it to the old way in which they did things. In existing markets, customers will more directly compare a new product to a competitive offering. Truly superior, differentiated products have a much higher success rate than "me-too" products.[3]

Product Life Cycle

Product development is only the first step in the so-called product life cycle. Figure 4-3 reflects a prototypical temporal pattern in a product's sales and profits over its life cycle.

The figure distinguishes five stages:

1. Development: In the period before the product is introduced, investments increase, while sales are nonexistent.

2. Introduction: When the product is launched in the marketplace, initial sales growth is typically slow, but marketing expenses and other costs are high, leading to negative profits. Customers that enter in this stage can be characterized

FIGURE 4-3

Product life cycle

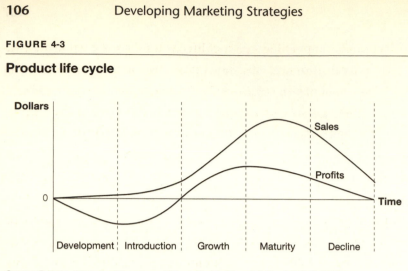

Source: P. Kotler, *Marketing Management* (Upper Saddle River, NJ: Prentice Hall, 2003).

as "innovators." The firm's primary marketing objective in this stage is to create product awareness and trial.

3. Growth: Sales rapidly rise in the growth stage. The early adopters now join the firm's customer base, and this growing market acceptance goes along with economies of scale and rising profits. In this stage, amid a growing number of competitors, the firm is primarily focused on maximizing its market share.

4. Maturity: Sales levels peak in the maturity stage, but sales growth slows down as the market saturates and competition further increases. It becomes less efficient to reach new customers and more difficult to effectively market the product. As a result, profits level off. The firm's primary marketing objective is to maximize profits while defending market share.

5. Decline: In the final stage, sales fall, and profitability virtually disappears. Some competitors may exit the market at this stage. The firm's objective is to reduce expenditures and milk the brand.

Naturally, in practice, product life cycles show a great deal of variety, as a result of both decisions taken by the marketer and other factors. For example, some products are characterized by fashions or fads that lead to a sharp peak in sales irrespective of the stage of the product life cycle. The context of the product introduction also plays a role. When a firm introduces an original product in a new market with a strong need for the product, the adoption process may be relatively quick. However, when firms must invest heavily in educating customers—for example, because significant competition exists, or because the product benefits are difficult to grasp—sales may not take off slower and profitability may be difficult to achieve.

Nevertheless, the product life cycle is a helpful tool for marketers seeking to understand the challenges and opportunities they face in managing a product. For each stage, they can map out the desired strategy regarding the marketing mix elements. As far as the product strategy is concerned, for instance, it is often useful to focus on offering a basic product in the introduction stage, add elements of the augmented product (such as customer service) and product extensions in the growth stage, extend and diversify the brand in the maturity stage, and prune the product or brand mix in the decline stage.

Managing Product and Brand Portfolios

The product life cycle concept indicates that it is critical for firms to manage its product and brand portfolios and to assess the manner in which its products interact within and across product lines. Effective firms have a detailed product development plan and a vision of where they want to be over time. That is not to say, of course, that plans should not be adjusted, but there must be a guiding philosophy on the desired extent of product proliferation, and how products will be added or deleted over time. In many industries, it is particularly useful to develop a product platform or template from which a family of products can be developed at low incremental cost.

The key reason to have a product line rather than a single product is to be able to better serve multiple market segments concurrently. In the ideal case, different products in the line or mix clearly map onto different target market segments.

Firms must avoid a situation in which little (or no) forward planning takes place and product lines evolve opportunistically. A lack of planning frequently results in a proliferated product line with poor coverage of the market segments. In addition, it often leads to a high level of competition between the company's own product offerings. Product planning should consider the extent to which demand for a new product will be truly incremental or will cannibalize the firm's existing products. Obviously, the relative profitability of the new and cannibalized items is a key factor in that analysis. If the unit margin on the new product is better than that of the cannibalized item (as is often the case when a company discovers a lower-cost way to bring the same level of functionality to market), this may not be as serious an issue. However, if the new item is less profitable than items it threatens to cannibalize (as is often the case when a company "trades down" its product line to reach more of the mass market), then careful consideration must be given to ways to limit the rate of cannibalization.

Over time, product lines typically proliferate, as it is usually more difficult for firms to delete an item from a line than to add one. Firms may expect strong negative reactions from customers and channel partners when a product is placed on the to-be-discontinued list. There is a real danger: customers may feel abandoned or poorly served by the company, and may even pressure the firm to take back previously sold items. Similarly, channel partners may "punish" the firm by allocating less shelf space to the firm's remaining products. However, a strong product line planning process includes a systematic investigation of deletion opportunities to ease customers' decision making and improve the overall economics of the firm.

Summary

Product decisions start with an understanding of what the customer wants or needs and that the product or service offering is not the thing itself, but rather the total package of benefits obtained by the customer. When developing marketing strategy, marketers must consider their offering from the point of view of value delivered to the customer simultaneously and through a number of vehicles, such as the physical good itself, the brand name, the corporate reputation, presale customer education, postsale customer service, consumer financing, convenience, and reputation of the channel, be it direct from the manufacturer or through an intermediary. This area of marketing strategy development involves product line and brand-planning decisions, individual line item and brand decisions, new product development decisions, and product and brand life cycle management decisions.

Additional Readings on Product Portfolios and Brand Management

Aaker, David A., and Erich Joachimsthaler. "The Brand Relationship Spectrum: The Key to the Brand Architecture Challenge." *California Management Review*, July 1, 2000. This article introduces a powerful brand architecture tool, the "brand relationship spectrum," to help brand managers employ insight and subtlety to subbrands, endorsed brands, and their alternatives.[4]

Cravens, Karen S., and Chris Guilding. "Strategic Brand Valuation: A Cross-Functional Perspective." *Business Horizons*, July 15, 1999. The authors compare and contrast such methods of brand valuation as cost-based approaches, market-based approaches, income-based approaches, and formulary approaches.

Quelch, John A., and David Kenny. "Extend Profits, Not Product Lines." *Harvard Business Review*, November 2005. Quelch and Kenny describe how marketing managers can sharpen their product line strategies by improving cost accounting, allocating resources to popular products, researching consumer behavior, coordinating marketing efforts, working with channel partners, and fostering a climate in which product line deletions are not only accepted but also encouraged.

Randall, Taylor, Christian Terwiesch, and Karl T. Ulrich. "Principles for User Design of Customized Products." *California Management Review*, August 1, 2005. This article defines the fundamental information-processing problem associated with user design of customized products, articulates five principles of user design, and outlines steps to improve user design systems.

Rust, Roland T., Debora Viana Thompson, and Rebecca W. Hamilton. "Defeating Feature Fatigue." *Harvard Business Review*, February 2006. This article explains how overloading products with features can erode profitability and how to avoid "feature bloat" or "featuritis" through more effective strategies.

Notes

1. Summary, Additional Readings, and Notes (except for the Snapple reference) were added to this chapter. They did not appear in the Class Note.

2. Snapple's parent company, Cadbury Schweppes, has a large number of other beverage product lines in its portfolio.

3. For in-depth analysis of disruptive products and services, see *The Innovator's Dilemma: When New Technologies Cause Great Firms to Fail* by Clayton M. Christensen (Boston: Harvard Business School Press, 1997) and *The Innovator's Solution: Creating and Sustaining Successful Growth* by Clayton M. Christensen and Michael E. Raynor (Boston: Harvard Business School Press, 2003).

4. For in-depth coverage, see D. A. Aaker and E. Joachimsthaler, *Brand Leadership: The Next Level of the Brand Revolution* (New York: Free Press, 2000).

Brand Valuation

RECOGNITION THAT BRANDS ARE ASSETS HAS A long history, but interest in the financial evaluation of brands is a more recent phenomenon—an outgrowth of the wave of mergers and acquisitions that began in the 1980s and in which brands often played a prominent role.[1] In addition to factoring into financial market transactions, economic evaluations of brands are frequently performed to serve other purposes, such as setting royalty rates in licensing brands, evaluating debt levels and risks, and estimating damages in trademark disputes.[2]

A variety of methodologies have been proposed and developed to meet this demand, and brand valuations are among the services regularly performed by several consulting firms.[3] One such firm is Interbrand Group plc., London. Birkin has described Interbrand's approach to assessing brand value. This appendix presents a simple illustration of how to apply Interbrand's method.[4] *Financial*

This appendix was written by Alvin J. Silk and originally published as "Brand Valuation Methodology: A Simple Example," Class Note 9-596-092 (Boston: Harvard Business School Publishing, 1996). It was lightly edited for consistency.

World (*FW*) annually publishes estimates of the value of more than two hundred brands that are based on a simplified version of the Interbrand methodology.[5] What follows is a summary of an example used by *FW* to illustrate its methodology.[6]

Briefly, a brand's value is taken to be the product of two quantities: (1) its annual net after-tax profits, adjusted to exclude the earnings expected for an equivalent unbranded product and averaged over time, and (2) a multiple (or discount rate), reflecting the brand's strength. The assessment of brand strength takes the following seven factors into account:

1. Leadership: ability to influence the market

2. Stability: ability to maintain a consumer franchise

3. Market: vulnerability of market demand to changes in tastes or technology

4. International scope: cross-national/cultural potential

5. Trend: long-term appeal to consumers

6. Support: strength of communications

7. Protection: security of the brand owner's legal or property rights[7]

The greater a brand's strength, the higher its multiple. Multiples range from six to twenty.

Estimating the Value of the Kellogg Brand

Kellogg's worldwide sales in 1994 were $5.5 billion with operating income of $1.0 billion. A summary of estimates of brand value for several well-known brands for the 1992–1994 period as reported in *Financial World* is presented in table 4A-1. The assumptions and calculations used to estimate the value of the Kellogg brand are shown in table 4A-2.

TABLE 4A-1

Estimates of brand value for selected brands (in millions of dollars)

Brand	1992	1993	1994
Coca-Cola	33,446	35,950	39,050
Marlboro	39,469	33,045	38,714
Pampers	5,924	5,732	5,919
Dewar's	NA	765	761
Black & Decker	NA	855	1,627
Kellogg	9,678	9,372	11,044
Kodak	NA	10,020	11,594

Source: Estimates reported in *Financial World*, September 1, 1993; August 2, 1994; and August 1, 1995.

TABLE 4A-2

Kellogg's estimated brand value (in billions of dollars)

Kellogg's 1994 worldwide operating income	$1.000
Less: estimated operating income of an equivalent unbranded product[a]	0.088
Kellogg's 1994 adjusted operating income	0.912
Kellogg's 1993 adjusted operating income	0.843
Weighted two-year average of Kellogg's adjusted operating income (relative weights 1994/1993 = 2/1)	0.889
Less: U.S. corporate tax: 34% × 0.889 =	0.302
Kellogg's net income, after tax: weighted two-year average	0.587
Estimate of Kellogg's "brand strength multiple"	18.76
Kellogg's estimated 1994 brand value: $0.587 billion × 18.76	$11.01

[a]To estimate the operating income of a nonbranded product line equivalent to Kellogg's:

1. Assume median capital/sales ratio for the processed food industry: 32%
2. Estimated capital investment required to produce sales of $5.5 billion for an equivalent nonbranded product: 32% × $5.5 billion = $1.76
3. Assume return on capital investment for an equivalent unbranded product: 5%
4. Estimated operating income for an equivalent unbranded product: 5% × $1.76 billion = $0.088

Source: Based on information presented in R. Meschi, "Value Added: Refinements in Our Brand Evaluation Methodology," *Financial World* 164 (August 1, 1995): 50–51.

Additional Resources for Assessing Brands[8]

Keller, Kevin L. "The Brand Report Card." *Harvard Business Review*, January 2000. Tuck School professor Kevin Keller lays out the ten dimensions that the strongest brands share. By grading a brand according to how well it addresses each dimension, managers can create a comprehensive brand report card. (Also available is a Brand Report Card exercise by Katherine N. Lemon, Elizabeth Bornheimer, and Kevin L. Keller.)

Keller, Kevin L., Brian Sternthal, and Alice Tybout. "Three Questions You Need to Ask About Your Brand." *Harvard Business Review*, September 2002. Managers should also consider the frame of reference within which the brand works, the features the brand shares with other products, and whether the differences are compelling.

Notes

1. P. Barwise et al., "Brands as 'Separable' Assets," *Business Strategy Review* (Summer 1990): 43–59.

2. See M. Birkin, "Why Brands Are Valued," *Admap* (March 1995): 18–19.

3. T. Ambler, "Brand Equity as a Relational Concept," *Journal of Brand Management* 2 (June 1995): 387; K. A. Longman, "Valuing a Brand," *Journal of Brand Management* 2 (April 1995): 273–279.

4. M. Birkin, "Assessing Brand Value," in *Brand Power*, ed. P. Stobart (New York: New York University Press, 1994), 209–222.

5. See, for example, K. Badenhausen, "Brands: The Management Factor," *Financial World* 164 (August 1, 1995): 50–69.

6. R. L. Meschi, "Value Added: Refinements in Our Brand Valuation Methodology," *Financial World* 164 (August 1, 1995): 52.

7. See Birkin, "Assessing Brand Value," and Meschi, "Value Added."

8. For in-depth coverage of branding, see D. A. Aaker's book, *Managing Brand Equity: Capitalizing on the Value of a Brand Name* (New York: Simon & Schuster, 1991), and K. L. Keller's textbook, *Strategic Brand Management*, 2nd ed. (Englewood Cliffs, NJ: Prentice Hall, 2002).

9. Additional Resources were added to this appendix. They did not appear as such in the Class Note. Notes 1 through 7 above appeared as footnotes in the Class Note but were lightly edited for consistency.

5.

Going to Market

A S DEFINED IN THE CHAPTER "MARKETING STRATEGY," the marketing channel is the set of mechanisms or the network via which a firm goes to market. Figure 5-1 shows four major classes of functions this network typically serves. The channel first must generate demand for a product or service and then fulfill that demand and provide for after-the-sale service. Finally, the channel often serves a useful function in transmitting feedback from the customer base back to the manufacturer.[1]

When a company thinks about going to market it must consider what each of the functions will specifically entail and who will do them—the manufacturer or a chosen partner such as a distributor or retailer. Very different go-to-market systems can be found in the marketplace. For example:

- Knoll Furniture, a leading maker of high-end office furniture systems, uses its own sales force to generate demand from large accounts. Demand fulfillment takes place through a dealer network.

This chapter was written by Robert J. Dolan and originally published as "Going to Market," Class Note 9-599-078 (Boston: Harvard Business School Publishing, 1999). It was lightly edited for consistency.

FIGURE 5-1

Market channel tasks

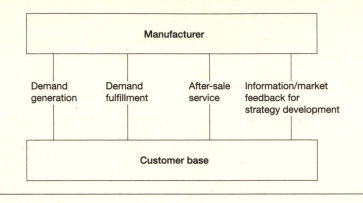

- Avon Products generated $5 billion in sales in 1997, selling through 2.6 million sales representatives worldwide. Selling mostly cosmetics and fragrances, these reps are independent agents, not employees of Avon, who work part-time selling to female customers on a door-to-door basis.

- Tupperware follows a similar direct selling model for its food storage containers, utilizing 950,000 independent Tupperware consultants worldwide. These consultants sell via the "party plan" in which potential customers gather at the home of a hostess for refreshments, product demonstration, and product ordering.

- The Gap, Inc. designs all its own products, which it sells through more than 2,000 company-owned retail stores. It also deals in electronic retailing, opening the Gap Online store at www.gap.com. It outsources manufacturing, purchasing from 1,200 suppliers, but manages the going-to-market phase entirely itself.

- BMW, on the other hand, goes to market through partners, about 300 franchised dealers selling its automobiles in the

United States. The dealers and BMW share responsibility for demand generation. BMW designs and implements national advertising. Dealers provide for product display and convenient testing by customers. Dealers fulfill demand, delivering vehicles to customers, and provide local after-the-sale service.

- Compaq Computer sells primarily through third-party resellers. A systems integrator may obtain a Compaq computer and package it with other equipment to sell a system to a customer. Like the Gap, Compaq has a direct online selling capability.

Due to differences in the market situation, these manufacturers have seen fit to go to market in different ways.

The go-to-market approach may vary even within a firm for different customer segments. The firm may choose multiple channels. The Gap's setup of its electronic store on the Web is an example of this strategy. The not-time-pressured customer who enjoys shopping visits the company store at the mall, while the time-pressured shopper visits the online store. A given individual may find a different channel more efficient depending on the buying occasion—for example, a new sweater may merit a store visit, and a simple blue jean replenishment order for a known size and style may be best handled on the Web.

This chapter expands on the treatment of marketing channels in "Marketing Strategy." As noted there, and suggested by these examples, the two key issues in going to market are (1) designing the network (i.e., who is on the team and what each should do) and (2) managing the network. In the short term, this means figuring out how to motivate each team member to do the desired tasks. In the longer term, it means determining how to evolve and hold the system together in light of new products, how to develop the customer base (e.g., formation of buying groups), and how to use new communications technologies such as the Internet.

Channel Design

Not too long ago, the most common approach to channel design was a very simple one. It was made simple by two assumptions that are no longer tenable. The first was that you should reach all your customers the same way. The thinking was that dual-distribution schemes were unworkable (e.g., selling to some customers via a company sales force and to others via a distributor was asking for trouble); similarly, having your own retail store on the streets of Manhattan and relying on retailers for coverage of less densely populated areas was a route to continual conflict. The second assumption was that if you signed up a channel partner between yourself and the end user, you basically did a "baton pass" of the entire marketing job to that intermediary. A manufacturer using a distributor shipped product to that distribution, and the distributor was responsible for generating leads, qualifying customers, conducting the selling process, closing the sale, and delivering the product.

Now, however, the fragmentation of most firms' customer base has ruled out the one-size-fits-all channel strategy. For example, the boom in working at home has created a home office furniture business that those traditionally supplying large corporations find too significant to ignore. And it's obvious that companies shouldn't sell to American Express and one of its cardholders in the same way. New customers have different information needs from the installed base. At the same time, the options for reaching customers have expanded. Quick delivery of a product in response to a customer used to necessitate a distributor holding stock in local areas. Now the same can be provided by a single inventory point and a contract with Federal Express.

Instead of a one-size-fits-all, baton-pass mentality a company must break up "the market" into segments and "the marketing job" into its component pieces, using the concept that different mechanisms could be the best way of accomplishing certain tasks for certain segments.

The first step in channel design is to ask: (1a) what segments of the market should be considered, and then (1b) for each segment individually, what tasks must be performed and what are the feasible options for doing them? Moriarty and Moran set out a process for designing "hybrid systems" in which different tasks are accomplished by different players.[2]

In their example, they break demand generation down into four subtasks:

1. Lead generation

2. Lead qualification

3. Presale activity persuading target customer

4. Closing the sale

Their terminology for the two other key channel tasks is:

1. Postsale service

2. Ongoing account management

Using these basic tasks as a guide, one should develop a more specific set for each segment. For example, consider an office furniture manufacturer. As step 1a, the manufacturer elects to serve both the at-home segment and the large corporate segment. See figure 5-2 to learn the tasks needed to accomplish obtaining and maintaining the at-home buyer.

Moriarty and Moran suggest using the "hybrid grid" to support decision making on how tasks should be accomplished. The grid, as shown figure 5-3, is a map of the tasks to be accomplished as the columns and the ways of possibly accomplishing the task as the rows. Each column has one X placed in it to show the mechanism via which the task moving the customer through the purchase process may be affected.

At the start of the process, one should think expansively about the possible matrix rows (i.e., the options for providing for specific

FIGURE 5-2

Tasks required to obtain and to maintain "at-home" buyers

Preliminary	1. Attract attention as potential supplier
	2. Position company as ergonomic experts and one-stop shop for all needs (desk, chair, files, etc.)
Present the offering	3. Describe available products
	4. Demonstrate products
	5. Communicate prices
Sale to install	6. Accept order; provide means of tracking order status
	7. Provide rapid delivery (at-home buyer typically does not preplan)
	8. Enable easy assembly/installation
Postsale	9. Manage warranty service issues
	10. Sell accessories
	11. Extend credit

FIGURE 5-3

The hybrid grid

Marketing channel/method	Tasks to be accomplished				
	1	2	3	4	. . . . . .
A.		X			
B.	X				
C.			X		
D.				X	
.					
.					
.					

Source: R. T. Moriarty and U. Moran, "Managing Hybrid Marketing Systems," *Harvard Business Review*, November–December 1990.

task accomplishment). For the furniture seller, for example, task 4 ("demonstrate products") may initially suggest the need for a customer visit to a retail outlet. But, with new technology, perhaps an adequate "demonstration" could be done virtually on the Web. Or, if convinced of the power of an in-home demonstration, one could induce a sale by offering free delivery and returns if the product is not satisfactory.

Imagine that the best plan for accomplishing the eleven at-home buyer tasks is as shown in table 5-1. In this model, the firm did not pass the baton of its marketing job to another entity. Rather, it kept nine of the eleven functions itself and outsourced two: task 6 to Federal Express and task 11 to the credit card companies.

Obviously, the approach for the furniture maker to serve a large corporate account moving into a new headquarters building would be quite different. The economics of a large order allow for different selling techniques, but more fundamentally the tasks that must be accomplished are different. For example, they might be these fourteen tasks:

1. Get on short list for this job (any account of this size would already be aware of the company and its positioning vis-à-vis competitors)

2. Present the product line

3. Demonstrate company ability to customize a solution to client's needs

TABLE 5-1

Plan for accomplishing at-home buyer tasks

Tasks 1–2	Advertising in mass magazines
Tasks 3 and 5	Web site preferred; catalog for those without Web access
Task 4	Free in-home trial
Task 6	Limit variety available to allow delivery from inventory and use Federal Express or other express shipper
Tasks 7–9	Company telemarketing/800 number
Task 10	Direct mail (using addresses from shipping data)
Task 11	MasterCard/Visa

4. Work with client's architect/designer to specify furniture solution, including mock-up of furniture at customer location

5. Negotiate price/terms

6. Facilitate disposal of old furniture

7. Accept order

8. Work with other vendors to develop installation plan

9. Respond to changes made to order from time of order to delivery

10. Deliver and install systems

11. Maintain systems

12. Sell accessories and additional systems

13. Upgrade as new products are introduced

14. Extend credit

Again, the hybrid grid should be used to specify the possible mechanisms to accomplish these tasks. This helps to show key handoffs and cooperations. For example, step 2 may be best achieved by a visit to the local dealer showroom. Then steps 3–7 are to be accomplished by the company salesperson without any dealer input.

This example is typical in the sense that the different segments have very different marketing systems set up to serve them. In the case here, the at-home buyer and large corporation are so different that the systems are unlikely to come into conflict with one another. They could, if the firm made the mistake of offering a lower price on an item on its Web site for the at-home buyer than it offered to the customer buying large quantities of the same item. But generally, this example's two segments seem to be distinct enough that the manner of servicing one would have little impact on the other. Such is not always the case, however. Once the tentative assessments have been made at the segment level, they must be rolled up into a system view for potential channel conflicts.

As an example, figure 5-4 depicts a marketing system in which the manufacturer has a multiple channel strategy (i.e., it goes to market through its own sales force calling on large accounts and uses distributors to call on smaller accounts). Potential conflict area 1 is that between the company sales force and distributors. A distributor may regard a potential account as rightfully the distributor's to serve and resent the loss in margin opportunity due to the company's serving the large customers directly.

A specific example of this type of conflict in channels was Compaq's November 1998 decision to sell computers directly to small-business customers via the Internet. The new Prosigna line was offered via the Compaq DirectPlus online service. Compaq was already selling through forty-four thousand dealers and described the addition of the direct channel for the segment as a melding of traditional sales channels and the Internet, offering customers a choice. However, one commentator noted, "Customer choice is great, but can they really continue this highwire tension between channel sales and the direct model?"[3]

FIGURE 5-4

Three types of channel conflict

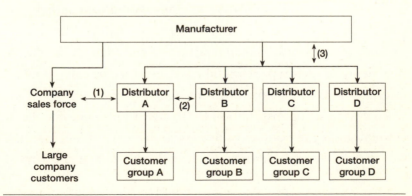

In the Compaq case, the potential conflict stemmed from a change in the marketing channel. Dealers felt that they were entitled to the customers and that Compaq was now bypassing them and reaching customers directly. Conflict issues of type 1 can arise even at the setup of a marketing channel from scratch. Often a firm perceives two segments in the market: a price-sensitive one and a service-sensitive one. In an attempt to serve the price-sensitive segment, it distributes through no-frills channels that keep costs low by performing little market education and compete on price. The service-sensitive segment is to be served in a higher-cost, more service-intensive channel. Conflicts arise when there is "leakage" between the segments. For example, customers get their education needs met in a specialty store and then go to buy at a discount outlet or mail-order. Some service customers will not desert their channel but use the price they come to see in the no-frills channel as a negotiating device with the full-service provider.

Conflict area 2 shown in figure 5-4 is between the same type of entities in the channel structure, here two distributors. In the figure, the manufacturer has chosen to have four independent distributors. This is the company's answer to the question of channel breadth—that is, how intensely to cover the market at a particular stage in the channel. Real-world examples were presented earlier.

For example, Tupperware had to figure out how many sales consultants it should have running parties. Too few would not generate enough sales for the company; too many would have individuals competing directly for too small a business potential. The Gap set its strategy of owning its own retail stores and then had to decide how many of each type it would have. Even in the same product category, firms can choose different intensity levels. For example, when Nissan set up distribution for its new Infiniti automobile, it chose to limit the number of dealers to just over 100 despite the fact that BMW and Mercedes each had over 350 in the United

States. The basic alternatives with respect to channel breadth or intensity of market coverage are:

- Exclusive distribution

- Selective distribution

- Intensive distribution

In **exclusive distribution**, the manufacturer establishes only one reseller in each region to carry the product. Yamaha pianos are an example of this policy. Exclusivity is granted by the manufacturer in the hope that it will induce strong selling support by the reseller. The cost is that, with an exclusive policy, consumers must be willing to seek out the one outlet in their area carrying the brand.

The middle ground between exclusivity and seeking the maximum coverage possible is **selective distribution**. In selective distribution, there is more than one reseller, but a limited number, in each market. Selective distribution is practiced by many higher-end clothing manufacturers, such as Perry Ellis and Bally. The purposive limiting of the number of outlets is intended to increase the support the reseller provides the brand over the case of intensive distribution. Having more than one outlet is intended to increase shopping convenience over exclusive distribution.

Finally, many manufacturers try to place their products with as many resellers as possible. For some markets, it is believed that "share of space" (i.e., retail shelf space) delivers "share of market," and, thus, the objective is to be as widely and intensively distributed as possible. Gillette razor blades, Kodak film, and Budweiser beer are examples of **intensive distribution** at the retail level.

Note that it is not necessarily the case that the more outlets the product is in, the better off the manufacturer is. Moving from exclusive to intensive trades off reseller support in return for easier availability of goods for the consumer.

As is usually the case in marketing, an analysis of consumer behavior is the primary input into the resolution of the channel breadth issue. Consider three examples:

1. Shaving cream: Shaving cream is a frequent purchase for the majority of adult males. The acquisition of a new can is a routine and unexciting event. Since the buyer most likely thinks there are a number of acceptable shaving creams, the manufacturer sees convenient availability as critical.

2. Television set: A television set is a relatively infrequent purchase of considerably greater expense than shaving cream. When the decision is made to buy a television set, several members of the family get involved—checking *Consumer Reports* and newspaper ads, shopping around, and generally gathering information appropriate to the importance of the decision. Since consumers do shop around, rather than just visit the most convenient outlet and buy there, there is no need for the manufacturer to be in every outlet. In fact, being in every outlet would likely be a mistake if the family relied on the retail salesperson for information. Intensive distribution is justified for the shaving cream because the only retail support required is shelf space. However, when strong point-of-purchase personal selling is required, going beyond selective distribution would jeopardize the required support.

3. Automobile: For some makes, the consumer behavior may be like that just described for television sets. However, for a specialty item, such as a Porsche Boxster, it is likely that the purchaser has a very strong brand preference even before the acquisition process begins. Thus, convenience of outlet is not a consideration, and the buyer will go just about anywhere to get the brand. Since the car is purchased infre-

quently and is an extremely important purchase, the buyer can behave this way. In this event, the permissibility of relatively inconvenient outlets indicates exclusive distribution. (Note that some provision may have to be made for less than exclusively distributed warranty servicing of the car.)

These examples illustrate a categorization of goods frequently used in marketing. The shaving cream, television, and exotic car represent a "convenience good," a "shopping good," and a "specialty good," respectively. Of course, no item can be definitely classified as any one of these three types for all consumers. However, the following is a useful guideline:

Convenience good $\longrightarrow$ Intensive distribution

Shopping good $\longrightarrow$ Selective distribution

Specialty good $\longrightarrow$ Exclusive distribution

Turning back to the conflicts of figure 5-4, the first two types of conflict shown are horizontal, and the third is vertical (i.e., between successive levels in the marketing system). Channel members are interdependent in the sense that their joint efforts determine the level of sales achieved for the product. Consequently, there is a natural incentive to cooperate. However, there is also an inherent stimulus to conflict. Each party would like to see the other do more to improve the sales situation. A distributor wishes the manufacturer would spend more on national advertising to set the stage better for the distributor's sales force as it calls on customers. The manufacturer wishes that the distributor would invest in better training for the sales force and outfit the salespeople with state-of-the-art selling tools.

Researchers have identified the major sources of conflict as parties' differences in:

- Goals

- Understanding of proper scope of activities

- Perceptions of reality[4]

An obvious difference in goals between a manufacturer and a distributor is each is focused on its own sales, not the other's. The manufacturer may see an opportunity to expand its sales by opening up a new channel like the Internet. The distributor sees this as cannibalizing sales it would otherwise make. A distributor typically incorporates the manufacturer's product with lines from other manufacturers. To suit the distributor's purpose, the line may take on a strategic role that does not serve the best interests of the manufacturer.

These conflicts are natural occurrences between two business entities each trying to serve its stakeholders. Contracts can be set up to mitigate goal incompatibility problems. These might specifically address what each party will contribute to the joint effort, how the effort will be monitored, and the division of the system profits contingent upon inputs each party provides.

The second related major source of conflict is differences in understanding about the scope of activity—namely, (1) the functions that each party will carry out and (2) the target population for whom the parties will perform these functions. For example, a distributor may see it as the company's job to open new accounts that are then turned over to the distributor for service; meanwhile, the company expects the distributor sales force to be cold calling and can't understand why the customer list is not seeing new additions each month.

A second key scope issue is the population served, defined either geographically or by account type. This is basically the issue of who owns the account. If a copier manufacturer serves the city of Boston direct (through its own sales force) but has a distributor for outlying districts (e.g., Cambridge), whose account is Harvard Business School, physically located in Boston but part of Harvard University, based in Cambridge? The hybrid grid model described earlier can be a useful mechanism for getting all channel partners to understand how the overall system is designed to work and their roles in it.

The third source of conflict is simply different perceptions of the reality of a situation. For example, the distributor with its sales force on the street every day may see the performance gap that has developed in the eyes of customers between the manufacturer's product and those of competitors. But the manufacturer still believes it is delivering superior quality. As another example, the manufacturer, tracking unit sales, sees a downward trend while the distributor sees a rapidly declining overall market in which it has more than held market share for the manufacturer.

Effective channel management requires recognition of these potential threats to the system's working as it should. Some issues can be avoided by carefully drawing up a specific understanding about roles, duties, performance measurement, and payoffs. The key is to have all members see the interdependence of system members and to arrange communications and contracts so that all parties perceive a fair return to their value added to the system.

Summary

This chapter covered the two major decisions in channels—namely, channel design and channel management. It broke down demand generation into general phases, namely lead generation, lead qualification, presale persuasion of target customers, deal closure, postsale service, and ongoing account management. Marketing system design issues are critical and can be a source of competitive advantage. Some companies are, in fact, defined more by their marketing system than their products. For example, the innovation and phenomenal success of Dell, Inc. was not so much in its range of computer systems and services but in its ability to customize each product to customer requirements and deliver directly to the end user and as in its direct distribution. A marketing system also must be examined for its adaptability to new market opportunities and new technologies. Because channels involve complex legal relationships, they can be difficult to adjust, and flexibility should be a criterion in judging a proposed structure.[5]

Additional Readings on Channel Management and Go-to-Market Strategy

Aaker, David A., and Erich Joachimsthaler. "The Lure of Global Branding." *Harvard Business Review*, November 1999. The authors offer four prescriptions for companies seeking to launch global brands.

Anderson, Rolph, Rajiv Mehta, and Alan J. Dubinsky. "Will the Real Channel Manager Please Stand Up?" *Business Horizons*, January 15, 2003. Based on a national study and a systematic review of the literature, this article identifies who actually manages go-to-market channels.

Dell, Michael, and Joan Magretta. "The Power of Virtual Integration: An Interview with Dell Computer's Michael Dell." *Harvard Business Review*, March 1998. This McKinsey Award–winning article explores Michael Dell's highly innovative way of combing the individual pieces of Dell Computer's strategy—Dell's customer focus, supplier partnerships, mass customization, just-in-time manufacturing—where technology-enabled coordination across company boundaries has achieved new levels of efficiency, productivity, customer satisfaction, and shareholder value.[6]

Nunes, Paul F., and Frank V. Cespedes. "The Customer Has Escaped." *Harvard Business Review*, November 2003. The authors urge companies to design pathways across channels to help their customers get what they need at each stage of the buying process, designing one's go-to-market strategy for buyer behaviors, not customer segments.

Notes

1. Additional Readings were added to this chapter. They did not appear in the Class Note. Notes 2 through 4 below appeared as footnotes in the Class Note but were lightly edited for consistency.

2. R. T. Moriarty and U. Moran, "Managing Hybrid Marketing Systems," *Harvard Business Review*, November–December 1990.

3. R. Guth, "Compaq Goes After Direct-Sales Model," *Infoworld*, November 16, 1998.

4. L. W. Stern, A. I. El-Ansary, and A. T. Coughlan, *Marketing Channels*, 5th ed. (Englewood Cliffs, NJ: Prentice Hall, 1996).

5. To explore this topic further, see V. K. Rangan, *Transforming Your Go-to-Market Strategy: The Three Disciplines of Channel Management* (Boston: Harvard Business School Press, 2006).

6. For in-depth coverage, see M. Dell with C. Fredman, *Direct from Dell: Strategies That Revolutionized an Industry* (New York: HarperCollins, 2000).

6.

Marketing Communications and Promotions

MARKETING IS THE PROCESS THROUGH WHICH A firm creates value for its chosen customers by meeting those customers' needs.[1] The firm is then entitled to capture a portion of the created value through pricing. But before this can happen, the consumer not only must be aware of the product's existence but also must sufficiently value it to choose the firm's product over competitive products or over not buying at all. This is where marketing promotions come into play.

The chapter "Marketing Strategy" set out the six *M*s model for communications planning (see figure 6-1). The first three elements

This chapter was written by Marta Wosinka and originally published as "Marketing Promotions," Class Note 9-506-028 (Boston: Harvard Business School Publishing, 2005). She based part of the material on an earlier note, R. J. Dolan, "Integrated Marketing Communications," Class Note 9-599-087 (Boston: Harvard Business School Publishing, 1999). It was lightly edited for consistency.

FIGURE 6-1

Six *M*s model for communications planning

1. **Market**	To whom is the communication addressed?	
2. **Mission**	What is the objective of the intervention?	Strategy
3. **Message**	What are the specific points to be communicated?	
4. **Media**	Which vehicles will be used to execute on the goals?	
5. **Money**	How much will be spent in the effort?	Implementation
6. **Measurement**	How will impact be assessed after the campaign?	

of that model deal with overall strategic goals, while the last three delve into implementation.

Understanding the Buying Process

Resolving the strategic component of the promotions plan begins with a careful analysis of the target consumers' decision-making process (DMP). Although the ultimate goal of a marketer is to have a consumer buy the firm's product or service, there is typically a sequence of steps a consumer goes through leading up to the actual purchase. A valid communications goal can be to move the customer from one of these early steps to the next. A general model of the steps that a consumer may go through is called the hierarchy of effects model.

The steps presented in figure 6-2 can be described in terms of the type of response required from consumers to move along in the hierarchy: cognitive, affective, and behavioral. In the cognitive stage, the communications job is to put some facts into the mind of the potential consumer. The first step is to make a consumer *aware* of the existence of the product and then build *knowledge* by conveying some information about it. The remaining steps in the affective stage are to move from *liking* to *preferring* the product over

FIGURE 6-2

Hierarchy of effects

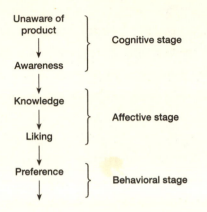

Source: R. J. Dolan, "Integrated Marketing Communications," Class Note 9-599-087 (Boston: Harvard Business School, 2000).

others and finally having a strong intent or conviction to buy it. The process advances to the behavioral stage that culminates in a repeat purchase of the product.

There is no one universally applicable model of the purchase process. The level of involvement and hedonic dimensions of the product will necessarily change the hierarchy of effects through the elimination, addition, or reversal of different stages. In addition, the time between purchases can affect whether the last stage in figure 6-2 is relevant. For instance, real estate developers will not concern themselves with getting the family that just bought one of their properties to purchase from them again when the family moves to another state ten years from now. In contrast, firms may be very concerned about the purchase-repurchase cycle if the stream of income a customer provides is high relative to any individual purchase (e.g., prescription drugs for chronic conditions or household cleaning supplies).

Major Promotional Tools

Marketers have at their disposal a large and ever-growing number of promotional vehicles. These tools differ in their ability to obtain feedback, to customize and control the message, and in the demands they put on the firm in terms of financial commitments and development of specific competencies.

Advertising

Most broadly defined, **advertising** refers to the paid placement of announcements and persuasive messages in time or space to inform and/or persuade members of a particular target market or audience about a product, service, organization, or idea. Within advertising, one can distinguish among many tools, which differ on two dimensions: level of feedback and customization (see figure 6-3). Some communications options, such as television, are lim-

FIGURE 6-3

Characteristics of advertising options

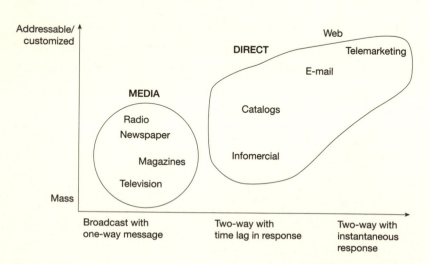

Source: R. J. Dolan, "Integrated Marketing Communications," Class Note 9-599-087 (Boston: Harvard Business School, 2000).

ited to transferring broadcast, one-way messages. Other media alternatives, like telemarketing, allow for instantaneous feedback. There is also a full spectrum of customization of the message. On the one hand, broadcast advertising on network television reaches millions of consumers with the same message. On the other hand, direct mail advertisements can customize or even personalize the message to new homeowners in particular zip codes.

In 2004, $141 billion was spent in the United States on media advertising. The largest share of expenditures was allocated toward television advertising ($58 billion), print advertising in magazines ($29 billion), and print advertising in newspapers ($28 billion).[2] Although overall spending on advertising has been increasing, the popularity of the different media has been changing drastically for two reasons. First, technological innovation has created new channels of communication. Between 2003 and 2004, Internet advertising rose by 21 percent to $7 billion. Second, many of the traditional media are becoming increasingly saturated as firms' demand for advertising space grows faster than the supply of it. This increases across-the-board competition for the consumer's attention and makes it more difficult to break through the clutter. One place where this has been particularly prominent is television, where two-minute commercial breaks have been replaced with more frequent three-minute commercial runs increasingly filled with fifteen-second ads.

Personal Selling

Personal selling is a highly flexible yet expensive form of marketing communication. It allows for instantaneous feedback, great customization potential, and therefore an ability to account for complex decision-making unit and DMP structures. This message flexibility comes at a cost—developing a qualified team of salespeople is sufficiently costly and challenging that having a great sales force is a definite strategic competency. In contrast to advertising, where the intensity level can be substantially adjusted from month to month, personal selling is a fixed resource in the short run, and suddenly ramping up marketing of one product necessarily comes at a cost of other tasks the salesperson is asked to do (this may include selling other products).

Sales Promotions

Because most products are sold through independent channels, channel partners can play a crucial role in influencing the consumer's buying process. Channels not only fulfill demand, but they are also involved in demand generation, after-sale service, and market feedback crucial for marketing strategy development. Manufacturers can use sales promotions to support or supplement channels in their marketing efforts on behalf of the product's manufacturer. There are two main types of sales promotions: consumer promotions and trade promotions.

Consumer sales promotions are designed to accomplish one or more of the following objectives: product trial; repeat usage of product; more frequent or multiple product purchases; awareness about a new/improved product; new packaging or different size packages; neutralizing competitive advertising or sales promotions; encouraging consumers to trade up to a larger size, more profitable line, or another product in the line. Consumer sales promotions often take the form of coupons, free samples, rebates, or premiums. A **rebate** returns a portion of the purchase price to the buyer in the form of cash. It commonly requires that a consumer sends proof of purchase and a rebate document to a processing center. A **premium** is an item of value, other than the product itself, given as an additional incentive to influence the purchase of a product.

Because consumer promotions induce consumers to seek out specific products or brands from the retail channels, they are com-

FIGURE 6-4

Push and pull strategies

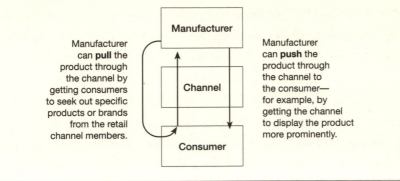

Manufacturer can **pull** the product through the channel by getting consumers to seek out specific products or brands from the retail channel members.

Manufacturer

Channel

Consumer

Manufacturer can **push** the product through the channel to the consumer— for example, by getting the channel to display the product more prominently.

monly referred to as "pull strategies" (see figure 6-4). The definition of *pull* is also commonly expanded to encompass advertising because that form of promotion is also meant to get the consumer to demand the product at the point of sale.

Trade promotions are financial incentives to the channel aimed at gaining support to carry an item, increase its visibility, or lower its price. Ultimately, the trade cares about product margins and the speed with which the product moves off its shelves. These financial incentives either directly increase retail margins or are passed through to consumers in the form of temporary price discounts, coupons, or placement in feature advertising in local Sunday newspapers. If trade promotion dollars are passed on to consumers, the retailer benefits through an increased rate at which the product moves off the shelves. Because trade promotions help the manufacturer to "push" products through the channel, they are commonly referred to as "push strategies."

Trade promotions take on many forms. Among the most prominent forms of trade promotions are discounts (e.g., volume discounts). Manufacturers may also pay the retailer **slotting allowance** fees to get distribution for a new product. These fees cover the various costs, such as making room for the product in the warehouse and on the store shelf, reprogramming the computer system to recognize the product's UPC code, and including the product in the retailer's inventory system. Manufacturers may also engage in **cooperative advertising** when they pay for local advertising or retail advertising placed by a local retail store in return for partial control over how product is featured. Restrictions may include that the product be the only one of its type in the ad, be the most prominently featured product, or not be advertised at a price below a certain level. In addition, manufacturers commonly pay for special displays placed at the end of store aisles or by the cash registers.

Indirect Forms of Promotion

There are numerous ways in which firms can affect the consumer DMP through third parties other than channels. In particular, communications received from other customers, experts, or media sources can influence a consumer's evaluation of a firm and its products. These partners in the communications effort are either minimally reimbursed for their effort (e.g., consumers may get T-shirts for talking to their friends about a product) or are unpaid and possibly not even explicitly aware of their promotional role.

The real or perceived impartiality of these parties can enhance the credibility of the message. But these indirect forms of promotion, albeit potentially powerful and inexpensive, provide limited control over the timing and the message associated with the intervention. Product placement in movies and television shows allows companies to create associations with the product; however, those companies do not necessarily control the context in which the product will be used. Just as with publicity, the desired outcome may be destroyed if negative associations are created. For example, while the Reese's Pieces candy greatly benefited through its prominence in the movie classic *E.T.*, the association of Arby's sandwiches with the killer in *Silence of the Lambs* did not create any such positive associations.

The marketer can attempt to influence coverage of its product by making information available through press releases or even by making the product available for test use to those who would then disseminate information about it to the market. Firms engage in public relations to build good relations with the company's various publics by obtaining favorable publicity, building up a good corporate image, and handling or heading off unfavorable rumors, stories, or events. However, disseminating this information may not always be easy. While the firm may know which reporters cover their industry and which experts matter, identifying influential consumers is perhaps the most challenging part of firms' efforts to tap into the word-of-mouth dynamics that may exist in the marketplace where the firm operates.

Integrated Marketing Promotions

There are two critical components in creating an integrated marketing campaign. The first one has already been alluded to earlier in this chapter—the firm must map the DMP to the selling process. The second critical step is to consider the internal consistency of these promotional tools.

Map the Buying and Selling Processes

By laying out the buying process of target consumer segments, firms have an opportunity to analyze each stage in isolation and to explore what makes the customer move from one stage to another. This can then be used to map a full strategy. For example, in early 1999, Mars introduced M&M Crunchy. The hierarchy of effects for this new candy joining Mars' lineup of plain, peanut, and peanut butter candies could be described as follows:

Unaware → Aware → Positive Attitude → Trial → Repeat

As is typical of a new product launch, the first task was to move the concentration of target consumers in the unaware state along to awareness and positive attitude. Given the broad target market definition, a spot on the Super Bowl was an ideal vehicle. Because consumers would likely move quickly through the hierarchy, programs were put in place to convert positive attitudes to trial at the point of purchase (at the store). Retail distribution was gained before advertising began and special retail displays and trade promotions were designed to increase salience at the point of sale and get the customers to try the product.

The consumer insight gained from a thorough DMP analysis can effectively suggest which media are most appropriate. For example, a U.S. manufacturer marketing detergent in Beirut learned that people hang their laundry to dry on their balconies. Given that the city of Beirut has multilevel buildings, the firm decided to use tops of buses as an advertising platform for the detergent. Along the same lines, Procter & Gamble used mirrors in women's bathrooms in bars to advertise its lipstick Outlast. The company was led to this idea through an insight that when women visit bar restrooms during their nights out, they stop by these mirrors to touch up their makeup. In both cases customer insight led these firms to new media solutions. These new media opportunities had the added advantage of being more distinctive than traditional media, although the novelty and the lack of clutter may eventually wear off in future campaigns, thereby decreasing their initially found effectiveness.

However, careful research into the consumer buying process need not necessarily lead one to the use of nontraditional media. Consider, for example, the case of Emerald, a California-based marketer of nuts for cooking that wanted to enter a snack nut category virtually owned by Planters. Emerald's marketing research revealed a key insight about the buying process—consumers did not believe or care about product differences between nuts because "a nut is a nut." Therefore, in a highly distinctive series of ads, great emphasis was placed simply on getting the name out. Strong brand linkage was achieved through highly entertaining mnemonics: "Egomaniacal Normans love Emerald Nuts" or "Encouraging Norwegians love Emerald Nuts." These fifteen-second ads were played at the beginning and the end of a commercial pod, therefore increasing the ability to create a strong brand linkage. The television medium was the best option for reaching a large and diverse target market, while the combination of sight and sound allowed the humor to come through easily.

Consider the Consistency

After considering how the firm can affect every step of the buying process, marketers should consider how these promotional tools interact with each other. In particular, every promotional tool conveys a message, whether intended or not. How these messages interact with each other ultimately affects the overall effectiveness of marketing promotions. For example, frequent sales may signal something different than an advertising campaign that presents the product as premium.

The need for message consistency goes beyond the marketing mix. In fact, the totality of the messages in the promotional mix—the pricing, the product's ability to deliver on the promised benefits, and the customer's experience at the point of sale (place)—contribute to how existing and potential customers perceive the product or service.

This discussion points to the need for consistency across promotional messages directed toward a given consumer segment. Firms should be cognizant of such conflicts in promotional messages in case the segments might get exposed to the conflicting messages. However, this is a matter of managing a conflict, not necessarily avoiding it entirely. A common solution is keeping a consistent overall positioning that is presented in mass media and customizing the message in media that do not overlap. For example, this potential conflict was behind Volkswagen's decision not to feature people in New Beetle ads so as not to associate the car with a specific demographic group. At the same time, salespeople at dealerships could customize the sales pitch—for example, by pointing out the flower vase to ex-hippies and the MP3 sound system to Gen-Xers.

Economics and ROI

Before a marketing strategy is fully mapped out, two other considerations come into play: how much to spend and whether this spending pays off. These considerations touch on the last two elements of the six *M*s analysis.

Sizing the Budget

The size of the marketing promotions budget is frequently a matter of great debate within companies. Many firms use simple rules of thumb to establish marketing spending levels. Some set budgets as a percentage of expected or previous year's sales. Others adopt a competitively based benchmark and spend to have a share of voice equal to share of market.[3] While these guidelines may be well suited as reality checks, the right way to approach the budget question is through what is called the "objective and task method"— that is, figure out what a firm must do to attain the firm's objectives and cost it out. Of course, one must make the business assessment that such expenditures will pay out in the end.

Allocation of the budget across promotional efforts is another contentious topic. Here again firms commonly use rules of thumb. What complicates this decision is the fact that different parts of an organization may control parts of the promotional mix. For instance, marketing, sales, and customer service often are separate departments with separate budgets and potentially divergent objectives. This kind of organizational misalignment can make optimal allocation difficult and also can result in poorly integrated promotional strategies if the DMP is not considered in its totality.

There are two overriding principles that should guide the allocation of promotional mix. First, the need to affect the various stages of the decision-making process should drive how the budget is allocated. In other words, which stages have a high throughput, and where does the DMP stop for a large share of consumers? For example, an introduction of one-a-day pill for hair loss prevention would likely be picked up by the media and may generate substantive word of mouth. However, the awareness-to-doctor-visit step may require a substantive marketing effort because the process between the onset of hair loss and the time when most customers act takes years. Second, the effectiveness of tools may vary, and the firm should understandably choose one that yields the highest impact per dollar spent. This leads to the final element of the six *Ms*—measuring effectiveness.

Measuring Effectiveness

An important part of marketing promotions planning is building in a mechanism to learn about the effects of the utilized efforts. This provides critical input into decisions on future spending levels, allocation of the budget across media, and specific communications messages. One reason why the average tenure of a chief marketing officer is only twenty-two months may be insufficient consideration for how to measure effectiveness of marketing promotions and the subsequent inability to show their results.

Clearly stating the objectives at the onset is a crucial first step. For example, if an objective is to "increase awareness of the three-year warranty on all of our products to 50 percent of the population by

June 1," research can be done to see whether the goal has been met. Because awareness is a cognitive effect that is not observable in the normal course of business activities, research such as a survey is an appropriate assessment tool. Another goal may be behavioral—for example, "get 25 percent of target population to try the product by June 1." Again, this can be assessed via market research. If a sales goal is specified—for example, "ship half a million cases by June 1"—one may only need to look at company records to assess whether the goal was accomplished.[4]

However, even with precisely stated goals, the dynamic nature of the marketplace can make a before-and-after comparison of sales results unreliable. For example, the effectiveness of Zocor's physician marketing may appear to have dropped in 1997 if one were not to account for the fact that a formidable competitor, Pfizer, entered the market with Lipitor and supported its new drug with a significant sales force effort. On the other hand, a cents-off price promotion may appear overwhelmingly effective during an economic recession because consumers' price sensitivity may rise during times of economic hardship.

Many models have been developed to account for such complexities, and companies often turn to vendors to conduct evaluations on their account. However, the importance of continual feedback on effectiveness calls for developing marketing research competencies in-house. Virtually every promotional tool lends itself to experimentation, where an intervention is introduced in one part of the market and withdrawn from another part, which then becomes the control group. In some cases, the opportunity cost of withdrawing the promotion from a subset of the market may be too high to warrant the strategy (e.g., when national advertising campaigns are involved). But experimentation can work well in tandem with current customer relationship management (CRM) efforts on the part of the firm because CRM databases can provide marketers with an incredible wealth of information that can be used to test promotional tools and customize these promotions toward the needs of select customer segments or even individual consumers.

Summary

This chapter introduces the major communications vehicles and the process by which marketers can combine them in an integrated marketing communications plan that may or may not include advertising and sales promotions. It covers the six-element (or six *Ms*) model of communications—namely, those elements of strategy (the market or audience to whom the communication is addressed, the mission or objective of the intervention, and the message or the specific points to be communicated) and those three elements of execution (namely, the media or vehicles used in implementation, the budget need to implement the effort fully, and the measurement system used to assess the campaign's effectiveness).

Additional Readings on Integrated Marketing Communications Strategy

Joachimsthaler, Erich, and David A. Aaker. "Building Brands Without Mass Media." *Harvard Business Review*, January 1997. Since costs, market fragmentation, and new media channels let customers bypass mass-media campaigns, the authors describe alternative brand-building approaches in the post-mass-media age.

Kassaye, W. Wossen. "Advertising and the World Wide Web." *Business Horizons*, May 15, 1997. This article provides an evaluation matrix for analyzing a company's or a brand's Web potential according to brand equity, global presence, and consumer characteristics, with emphasis on how to integrate Web advertising with existing media activities.

Raghubir, Priya, J. Jeffrey Inman, and Hans Grande. "The Three Faces of Consumer Promotions." *California Management Review*, August 1, 2004. This article presents a framework that examines the effect of managerially controllable actions—specifically, designing and communicating a sales promotion—on increasing the incentive for different segments of consumers to purchase a product.

Notes

1. Summary and Additional Readings were added to this chapter. They did not appear in the Class Note. The following references appeared as footnotes in the Class Note.

2. TNS Media Intelligence. "Ad$pender™" 2004 report (New York: TNS Media Intelligence, 2004).

3. Share of voice is the percentage of the product category marketing expenditures that is attributable to the firm. See also Dolan, "Integrated Marketing Communications."

4. Ibid.

Optimal Pricing

A S DESCRIBED IN THE CHAPTER "MARKETING STRAT-
egy," a firm's marketing efforts are directed toward
creating value for its chosen customers.[1] Understanding customers'
wants and needs is the foundation for building this value. In turn,
capturing that value falls to the marketing mix, commonly referred to as "the four *Ps*":

- Developing a *product* that satisfies those wants and needs

- Designing a *promotion* program that conveys the value of
  that product to customers

- Choosing a distribution program (i.e., *place*) that makes that
  product readily available

This chapter was written by Robert J. Dolan and John T. Gourville and
originally published as "Principles of Pricing," Class Note 9-506-021
(Boston: Harvard Business School Publishing, 2005). Professor Dolan prepared an earlier version of that note, "Pricing: A Value-Based Approach,"
Class Note 9-596-092 (Boston: Harvard Business School Publishing,
1999). It was lightly edited for consistency.

- Designing a *pricing* strategy that simultaneously creates a consumer's incentive to buy that product and the firm's incentive to sell that product

The first three of these marketing mix variables represent costs to the firm. Pricing's role in the marketing mix is to tap into the value created and generate revenues (1) to fund the firm's current value-creation activities, (2) to support research that will lead to future value creation, and (3) to generate a profit from the firm's activities.

A complete pricing program has many components. Consider the pricing decisions surrounding the launch of a new MP3 player. These might include:

- The unit price of the MP3 player to dealers and distributors

- The accompanying terms and conditions, such as:

  — whether and to what degree there will be a quantity discount

  — the schedule of payments (i.e., when payments are due)

  — whether there will be discounts for early payments or penalties for late payments

- The manufacturer's suggested retail price to the end consumer

- Whether there will be any consumer pricing promotions (e.g., mail-in rebates)

Such pricing decisions have broad implications for a firm's net income. If Coca-Cola, for example, could increase its prices by an average of 1 percent without affecting demand for its products, it would increase its net income by 6.4 percent. Thus, an average price increase of less than $0.01 on a can of cola would translate to an increase in net income of about $300 million. Further, Coke could achieve such an increase by raising the price to all of its consumers by 1 percent, by increasing the price to 20 percent of Coke's customers by 5 percent, or by increasing the price to 10 percent of Coke's customers by 10 percent.

Similar 1 percent price increases, if they did not negatively impact demand, would lead to increases in net income of 16.7 percent for Fuji Photo, 17.5 percent for Nestlé, and 26 percent for the Ford Motor Company. In fact, an average price increase of 1 percent would boost the net income of the typical large U. S. corporation by about 12 percent.[2] Thus, getting pricing right is a big deal.

However, getting price right is often an afterthought in many corporations. In particular, if:

Profits = (Unit Price – Cost of Goods Sold) × Unit Sales Volume

there often is more emphasis on the **cost of goods sold (COGS)** and **unit sales volume** parts of the profit equation than on **unit price**. These firms typically see price as "determined by the marketplace" or "something we really do not have much control over." One of the most common pricing strategies used by corporations remains "cost plus"—that is, determining the cost of goods sold and adding on a seemingly reasonable margin. Marketers with this reactive attitude typically miss great profit opportunities.

This chapter covers some of the important fundamentals behind optimal pricing. It builds on the appendix "Basic Marketing Mathematics," which presents the margin and break-even analysis useful in pricing decision making. The major sections of this chapter address the following:

- Understanding the value-pricing approach

- Assessing the product's value to customers

- Assessing price sensitivity

- Price customization

- Integrating price with the other marketing mix elements

The Value-Pricing Approach

The value-pricing approach to product pricing is driven by a small handful of factors, as shown in figure 7-1. One of these factors is the **objective value** the product delivers to the consumer.[3] Also called **true economic value**, this is a measure of the benefits that the product delivers to the consumer, regardless of whether the consumer recognizes those benefits.

A critical second factor is the **perceived value** of the product to a consumer. Perceived value is the value the consumer understands the product to deliver. Sometimes, a product's benefits are readily apparent to the consumer, and perceived value approaches objective value with little effort by the firm. Other times, a product's benefits are less obvious and need to be communicated by the firm to the consumer (e.g., via advertising or personnel selling). In such cases, the perceived value of a product typically falls well below its objective value.

FIGURE 7-1

Value-pricing "thermometer"

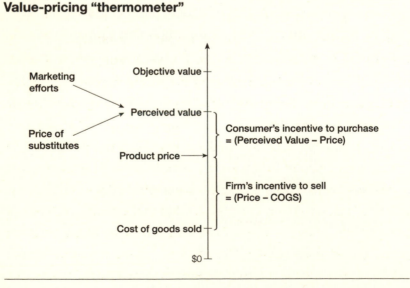

The perceived value of a product also can be influenced by the price of competing products or substitutes. Company A may develop a product that creates great objective value for consumers. Consumers may recognize this value and be willing to pay a high price to obtain the product. However, if Company B introduces an identical product at a much lower price, the perceived value of Company A's product will be reduced to the price of Company B's product.

Note that the perceived value of a product to a consumer *should* equal the maximum price that the consumer will pay for the product. Imagine a consumer who perceives the value of a DVD player to be $100. If it is priced above $100, the consumer has no incentive to buy the DVD player. If it is priced at $100 or less, however, the consumer always stands to gain from purchasing.

The last major component to the economic approach to pricing involves the firm's COGS. Just as the consumer requires an incentive to purchase a product, the firm requires an incentive to sell the product. To stay in business and make a positive return, a firm must charge a price that covers its cost of production.[4]

All of these economic factors come together to form the value-pricing approach to pricing. In optimally pricing a product, a firm is bound at the upper end by the consumers' perceived value for the product. This perceived value is influenced by the objective value of the product to the consumer, by the firm's marketing effort to communicate that objective value, and by the price of substitute products. At the same time, the firm is bound on the lower end by its COGS.

By pricing above the COGS and below perceived value, the firm has an incentive to sell the product, measured as price – COGS, and the consumer has an incentive to purchase the product, measured as perceived value – price. In value-pricing terminology, the firm has "created" value by offering a product that the consumer values at a price greater than the firm's COGS. In turn, by pricing between perceived value and COGS, the firm has "captured" some of that value for itself and has allowed consumers to capture the remainder.

Assessing a Product's Value to Customers

But how does a firm determine the objective and perceived value of a product to a customer? For determining objective value, firms often rely upon an understanding of the potential buyer's cost structure. For determining perceived value, firms often employ surveys in which potential buyers are asked directly about value. The following sections take a look at each, in turn.

Determining Objective Value Through Cost-Structure Studies

In a cost-structure study, one assesses the objective value or true economic value (TEV) of a product to a customer by understanding the competitive alternatives, the price and performance of those alternatives, and the buyer's costs.

TEV has two major components:

$$\text{TEV} = \text{Cost of the Next-Best Alternative} + \text{Value of Performance Differential}$$

First, if the buyer has several alternatives, the calculation has to be relative to the best alternative. For example, what is the objective value of a flight on the Delta Shuttle to a busy banking executive who needs to get from Boston to New York? One could calculate the TEV relative to going on the bus—but this leads to an irrelevant number, as the best alternative is the US Airways Shuttle, flying essentially the same schedule as Delta from the same airport. In this case, the value of the performance differential is likely to be very small, as there is little product differentiation. Hence, in this situation, the executive's TEV for Delta will be very close to US Air's price.

This approach is more useful when there is a performance differential to consider. A firm's product may be superior to the next-best alternative in some dimensions but inferior in others.

TABLE 7-1

Comparison of two products

	Next-best alternative	New product
Operating cost/hour	$10	$15
Probability of system crash	20% over one year	1% over one year
Price	$75,000	To be determined

Consider a next-best alternative and a new product with the characteristics shown in table 7-1.

Now consider a customer who needs such a system for a single year (after which it will be scrapped) and plans to use it for 2,500 hours over the course of that year. If the cost of a system crash to the buyer is $100,000 (e.g., the selling firm will bear the cost of any system crash after the first), the TEV for the new product can be calculated as:

TEV = Price of Next-Best Alternative + System Crash Savings
  – Added Operating Cost

= $75,000 + [.2(100,000) – .01(100,000)]
  – [(2,500 hrs x $15/hr) – (2,500 hrs x $10/hr)]

= $75,000 + $19,000 – $12,500 = $81,500

Thus, the objective value or **TEV** of this new product is **$81,500**, meaning a fully informed, rational consumer should be indifferent between the next-best alternative priced at **$75,000** and the new product priced at **$81,500**.

Determining Perceived Value

While it is important to understand the objective value a new product delivers, it is equally important to understand the value of that product as perceived by potential consumers. One common way to assess perceived value relies on survey methods. The most common of these is a direct-response survey, in which the respondent answers such questions as:

- What is the likelihood you would buy this product at a price of $25?

- At what price would you definitely buy this product?

- How much would you pay for this product?

- How much of this product would you buy at a price of $0.99?

- At which price difference would you switch from product A to product B?

Consider a major camera maker that used this method to set the price for a new camera. In a survey, a set of respondents were provided a description of the new camera and were asked to indicate their purchase intention on a seven-point scale, from "definitely not buy" to "definitely would buy." One-third of the respondents were told the camera would cost $150, one-third were told it would cost $80, and one-third were told it would cost $40. Results of the survey appear in table 7-2.

The fact that 47 percent of people responded with a 1, 2, or 3 ("probably would buy") for the $40 price (as opposed to only 19 percent for the $80 price) was instrumental in the firm's introducing the camera at a suggested retail price of $39.95.

Note that there are potential problems with direct-response surveys. For instance, they often induce an unrealistically high level of price consciousness in consumers. Similarly, given that consumers are only *asked* about their willingness to buy or to pay, and not actually required to spend their money, the results often paint an overly optimistic picture of a product's potential. Never-

TABLE 7-2

Survey results of purchase intent

	STATED PRICE OF CAMERA		
	$150	**$80**	**$40**
1. Definitely would buy	4%	5%	15%
2.	0%	0%	2%
3. Probably would buy	7%	14%	30%
4.	1%	2%	4%
5. Probably not buy	22%	34%	18%
6.	2%	2%	1%
7. Definitely not buy	65%	54%	30%

theless, such surveys are often a good first step in assessing perceived value.

Assessing Price Sensitivity

Another key element in determining price is price sensitivity, with that sensitivity varying across customers, across time, and across products. Consider an interventional cardiologist preparing to do surgery on a heart patient with a blocked artery. The best solution may be to insert a stent to hold back the plaque blocking the artery, allowing blood to again flow freely.

Given that there are three different stent manufacturers, how sensitive to price will the typical doctor be in this situation? Contrary to some expectations, the answer is "not very." First, given that this is a life-or-death procedure for the patient, product performance will be key. Second, the doctor is (hopefully) a very knowledgeable, sophisticated decision maker, aware of each stent's advantages and disadvantages for various types of blockages.

Third, the doctor may have more experience inserting one type of stent and would prefer not to shift from the usual brand. Finally, since the doctor is not paying for the stent, the doctor's sensitivity to price may be lower.

Much of this may seem pretty intuitive. But a systematic approach can be helpful in judging price sensitivity. Some of the major factors that influence price sensitivity are now discussed in turn.

The Magnitude of Price

Price sensitivity tends to be far greater in high-cost than in low-cost product categories. Thus, a 10 percent price differential on a sports car will be a far bigger deal than a 10 percent price differential on a tube of toothpaste. More broadly, price sensitivity is likely to increase as:

- The absolute dollar cost of the product increases. This is exemplified by the sports car and toothpaste example.

- The aggregate cost of ongoing usage increases. For example, a no-name golf ball may cost $1, and a high-end Titleist golf ball may cost $3. But a retired (not-so-good) golfer who plays two hundred times per year and loses an average of three balls per round may view this choice of golf ball as a $600 versus $1,800 decision, not a $1 versus $3 decision.

- The cost of that product increases as a percentage of the total cost. Dolan and Simon give the example of a chemical whose use accounted for 50 percent of the cost of producing insulation and 5 percent of the cost of producing polyesters.[5] A 10 percent price increase in the price of the chemical would increase the insulation maker's total cost by 5 percent, but it would increase the polyester maker's total cost by only 0.5 percent. As a result, the insulation maker was more sensitive to any price increase.

Who Pays?

Some products are paid for by the customer. Some are not. In the case of an automobile for personal use, for instance, the user of the car is also the payer. When the car is a company car, however, the user may bear none of the cost of that car. In some situations, the user of the product pays some, but not all, of the cost of a good, as is often the case with health insurance, where the employee pays some portion of the insurance and the company pays the remainder. Not surprisingly, to the extent that the user is responsible for the costs, the greater is that user's price sensitivity.

Competitive Factors

Competitive factors also impact price sensitivity.[6] Price sensitivity is higher to the extent that:

- The customer does not perceive significant differences in alternative products.

- It is easy to compare products and their prices. Some comparisons are apples to apples, as when two insurance policies each pay $1 million in the case of death. Such easy comparisons tend to highlight price. In contrast, price sensitivity is dampened when products are not easily compared, as when two disability policies vary in number of days covered, the frequency of payments, and the size of those payments. Similarly, price sensitivity is dampened when price is hard to compare, as when one vendor charges $0.10 per unit consumed while another charges $0.08 per unit plus a $10 monthly fee.

- It is easy for the decision maker to switch products. Difficulty in switching can arise for psychological reasons, such as when there is high perceived risk or there is a desire to stick with the familiar brand. It can also arise for economic reasons, as when there is a penalty for switching providers, when retraining or relearning is required, or when there is a loyalty program involved.

Price Customization

Given the value-pricing framework and the discussion of price sensitivity, one realizes that the perceived value of a product can vary significantly between individuals. For example, the latest golf-club innovation is more highly valued by someone trying to make a living as a professional than it is by an amateur. A number of factors cause value variation across potential customers, such as:

- Taste: Some people think Godiva chocolates are the greatest, while others would just as soon have a Hershey bar.

- Importance of performance: The experienced computer user values speed and storage more than the novice user.

- Ability to pay: A millionaire has more resources to pay for a high-definition television than a true television fan of lesser economic means.

- Intensity of use: A hands-free cell phone is more highly valued by a person using the device regularly as compared with those in "emergency-use-only" mode.

- Category knowledge: The experienced car buyer who has researched the market views the invoice price of a car as the appropriate benchmark, while the novice buyer views the sticker price of a car as the appropriate benchmark.

When value varies across customers, a pricing program should consider whether to customize price according to the value received, thereby charging a higher price to those who value the product more. Several means to customize price are:

- **Through the product line:** Firms can offer a high-end product with many features for the high-value customers and more basic models for the lower-value customers. For example, most new cars have a basic model, a number of intermediate models, and a fully loaded model. In turn, car buyers who place a higher value on basic transportation can choose the basic model, while those who value sunroofs and leather interiors can opt for the fully loaded model. Generally, the higher-featured items yield greater margins.

- **By controlling availability:** For example, a mail-order clothes company can send different catalogs (with different prices) to different customers depending on their past purchasing behavior. Delivering $1.00 coupons to selected households for redemption at the point of purchase is another method for selective pricing.

- **Through demographics:** Here, one looks for some characteristic of buyers that correlates with willingness to pay. For example, major movie theaters often offer discounts to children and senior citizens, anticipating that they will increase demand at nonpeak hours (e.g., afternoons for children, weekdays for senior citizens).

- **Through transaction characteristics:** Price is tied to the particular features of the transaction, such as how far in advance of consumption the product is purchased. For instance, in all likelihood, the customer who buys a plane ticket six months in advance has a far lower willingness to pay than the customer who buys a ticket three days in advance.

Integrating Price with Other Marketing Mix Elements

Finally, a key to effective pricing is to have a firm's pricing strategy in synch with the other elements of the marketing mix. Consider, for example, when Glaxo first introduced its ulcer medication, Zantac, at a substantial price premium over the incumbent product, Tagamet. In spite of being second to market, it was able to become the market leader because the product was superior *and* because Glaxo invested in the marketing effort necessary to communicate that superiority to potential consumers. In other words, Zantac had a high objective value, and Glaxo's marketing efforts were successful in raising potential consumers' perceived value toward that economic value. In turn, the high margins generated by the premium pricing funded that marketing effort.

Such pricing and marketing spending choices often are captured in figure 7-2.

As shown, two strategies are feasible. The company can follow a low-marketing-expenditure and low price (i.e., low relative to its

FIGURE 7-2

Pricing/marketing spending choices

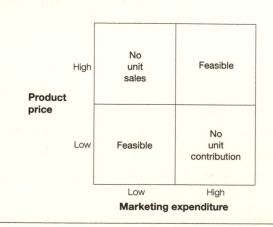

objective value) strategy. In such cases, the product's value must speak for itself. But, because of the low price, the hurdle for consumers to purchase is not high. Similarly, the company can follow Zantac's high-high strategy. In particular, it can invest in marketing to boost perceived value but price so as to capture the perceived value thereby created, attaining the margins necessary to fund the high-expenditure marketing effort.

Conversely, the other price and expenditure combinations are not feasible in the long term. High price and low marketing fails because the firm is not spending sufficient resources to convince potential consumers of the product's value. And low price and high marketing is not feasible because, while the high marketing expenditures may create significant sales, the low price results in no profits.

Legal and Ethical Issues

A discussion of pricing would not be complete without addressing several legal and ethical issues. In particular, pricing is an activity that can raise a number of legal and ethical issues whose resolution requires full consideration of the specific context.[7] This section will highlight several.

First, since price customization has been advocated in this chapter, it is important to state that it is not illegal to charge different prices for the very same product. Some individuals, however, view the practice as unfair. Some studies have, for example, shown that poor people, lacking mobility and access to alternative sources, pay higher prices for groceries in local supermarkets. Health advocates have criticized the high pricing of life-saving pharmaceuticals, such as AIDS drugs. Still others are critical of prices being high in one market and low in a neighboring region, as in the case of prescription drugs in the United States versus Canada. While such practices are not illegal, firms should be aware of their potential implications.

In contrast, questions of legality arise whenever pricing actions (including price customization) are seen as reducing competition. Pricing actions with potentially anticompetitive effects include:

- Predatory pricing: that is, pricing low for a time to drive a competitor from the marketplace

- Price fixing: setting prices in collusion with competitors

- Price maintenance: requiring that distributors or retailers sell only at a specified price (a firm *may* suggest reseller prices— as in the case of a manufacturer's suggested retail price—but *may not* require that such prices be maintained)

A company can be charged by the government and/or sued by customers or competitors for anticompetitive acts. The situation is not easy to navigate; for example, one observer noted, "When pricing tactics are illegal is not always clear. The laws themselves are vague."[8] Therefore, pricing practices should be subjected to both an ethical review and an informed legal review within the company before being implemented.

Summary

This chapter covered the basic principles of pricing, including the value-pricing approach to pricing, determining the product's value to customers, assessing the customer's sensitivity to price, leveraging price customization and discrimination, and integrating price with the other marketing mix elements. Considerations include a customer's taste, the importance of the product's performance, the customer's ability to pay, the intensity of usage, and the customer's knowledge of the product or service category. The chapter concluded by raising critical legal and ethical issues around a firm's pricing policies and practices.

Additional Readings on Pricing

Anderson, Eric, and Duncan Simester. "Mind Your Pricing Cues." *Harvard Business Review*, September 2003. The authors review several common pricing cues retailers use—sale signs, prices that end in nine, signpost items, and price-matching guarantees.

Cross, Robert G., and Ashutosh Dixit, "Customer-Centric Pricing: The Surprising Secret for Profitability." *Business Horizons*, November 15, 2005. Customer-centric pricing—the simultaneous and continuous assessment of product attributes, customer perceptions, and customer actions—enables companies to assess the value they create for and extract from customers.

Gourville, John T., and Dilip Soman. "Pricing and the Psychology of Consumption." *Harvard Business Review,* September 2002. The authors explain how the relationship between pricing and consumption lies at the core of customer strategy.

Sodhi, ManMohan S., and Navdeep S. Sodhi. "Six Sigma Pricing." *Harvard Business Review*, May 2005. The authors describe how a global manufacturer of industrial equipment recently applied Six Sigma to one major revenue-related activity, the price-setting process.

Vachani, Sushil, and N. Craig Smith. "Socially Responsible Pricing: Lessons from the Pricing of AIDS Drugs in Developing Countries." *California Management Review*, November 1, 2004. Corporate social responsibility has major implications for pricing decisions in some markets, and so this article offers lessons for managers in industries where socially responsible pricing may be an imperative.

Notes

1. Summary and Additional Readings were added to this chapter. They did not appear in the Class Note. The following references (excepting Note 6) appeared as footnotes in the Class Note.

2. R. J. Dolan and H. Simon, *Power Pricing* (New York: Free Press, 1997).

3. Given consumer heterogeneity, objective value and perceived value will tend to vary between consumers. For some consumers, these

values will be high; for others, they will be low or zero. For simplicity, this discussion ignores consumer heterogeneity for the moment and only consider the typical consumer.

4. For simplicity, this discussion ignores strategic reasons for pricing below cost, such as to build share or volume or to temporarily respond to a competitor's pricing efforts.

5. Dolan and Simon, *Power Pricing*, 130.

6. In the article "How to Fight a Price War" (*Harvard Business Review*, March–April 2000), A. R. Rao, M. E. Bergen, and S. Davis describe the causes and characteristics of price wars and explain how companies can fight them, flee them, or initiate them. The authors emphasize other options for protecting market share rather than price slashing, such as competing on quality instead of price; exposing the risks and negative consequences of a low-priced option; or involving interested third parties—governments, customers, and vendors—to help avert a price war. If a company chooses to compete on price, then it should use complex pricing actions—cutting prices in certain channels, introducing new products, or flanking brands—and not pursue simple tit-for-tat price moves.

7. See G. K. Ortmeyer, "Ethical Issues in Pricing," in *Ethics in Marketing*, ed. N. C. Smith and J. A. Quelch (Homewood, IL: Irwin, 1993); and T. Nagle and R. Holden, "The Law and Ethics," ch. 14 of *The Strategy and Tactics of Pricing* (Upper Saddle River, NJ: Prentice Hall, 1995).

8. Nagle and Holden, "The Law and Ethics," 386.

Part III

Implementing Marketing Strategies

Personal Selling and Sales Management

S ALES FORCES REPRESENT A MAJOR INVESTMENT
for many firms, accounting for 1 percent to 40 percent
of sales revenues.[1] Sales forces are employed by more than 70 percent of firms worldwide and account for approximately 10 percent
of the global workforce. In the United States, more than a trillion
dollars is spent annually on the nearly 12 percent of the total
workforce employed in full-time sales positions.

Because the success of any marketing strategy depends on implementation, the fortunes of firms that employ the personal selling approach can rise or sink with the performance of their sales
forces. Such firms need to carefully understand and manage their
salespeople (personal selling) and sales organizations (sales management). This chapter explores the unique role of a salesperson
(or sales rep) and management of the selling effort.

This chapter was written by Tom Steenburgh and Das Narayandas and
originally published as "Note on Personal Selling and Sales Management" Class Note 9-506-038 (Boston: Harvard Business School Publishing, 2005). It was lightly edited for consistency.

The Sales Representative: A Boundary-Spanning Role

Salespeople work on the boundary between a firm and its customers. They represent their company to, and are entrusted with, its most precious assets, its customers. A salesperson is to customers the physical embodiment of the firm; to the firm, the voice of the customer. This boundary-spanning role creates a unique tension. Situated between firm and customer, the sales rep is often called upon to manage conflicting rules, procedures, and task requirements (see figure 8-1).

Since the role of marketing is to help the field salesperson execute the boundary-spanning role as effectively as possible, the job of the marketing or product manager is to attend closely to whether and how marketing policies and programs help or hinder the sales rep.

The Sales Tasks Define the Salesperson

Sales reps' jobs are not stereotypical but change with the nature of the tasks that firms and customers expect them to perform. The best (and only) way to understand the jobs is to start with the lists of activities that sales reps are expected to perform.[2] These activities are called **sales tasks**.

FIGURE 8-1

The boundary role

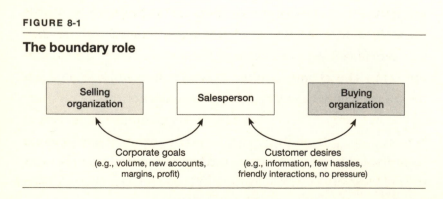

The "Going to Market" chapter covered demand generation, demand fulfillment, and after-sales service (or customer relationship management), the three buckets of channel functions. These buckets capture the variety of sales tasks that sales reps might perform. Based on the nature of the sales tasks to be performed, one can classify sales reps in the following manner.

Order takers. These reps are not expected to create demand for a firm's products; they wait for customers' orders. Their primary task is to satisfy customer demand. Order takers ensure that current customers have sufficient product quantities where and as needed. They might in some instances be expected to seek and pursue repeat or cross-selling opportunities. Examples of order takers are the person behind the counter at a fast food outlet or the post office, the floor salespeople in department stores, and so forth.

Order getters. Order getters obtain, retain, and increase business with customers. They pursue new and repeat business using creative sales strategies and well-executed sales approaches. Typical sales tasks of order getters include generating customer leads, providing information, persuading customers, and closing sales.

One of the commonly used categorizations in practice is to classify order getters as either "hunters" or "farmers." **Hunters** are salespeople who enjoy the thrill of identifying and selling new prospects—they like to hunt. **Farmers** are sales reps whose forte is the maintenance and growth of existing customer accounts—they take care of customers and generate new sales. These characterizations can be simplistic and often unfair. Hunters are more than just persistent door knockers with high ego-resilience that helps them bounce back from rejection and seek new opportunities, and farmers are more than just glorified customer service reps that only respond to customer demands. There is growing recognition that the skills required for both roles are the same. To be successful, hunters need to do more than go into a new account, make a dynamic presentation, and persuade customers to buy. They need to carefully plan the prospect they want to approach, get close to the prospect, understand that prospect's problems and needs, and offer an economically viable solution. These are the same activities that a farmer needs to do to successfully retain customers and grow the business.

Support Personnel

Salespeople whose job is primarily to facilitate the selling function can be further subdivided as follows.

Missionary salespeople. These sales reps distribute information about new goods and services and describe product attributes to and educate customers. They do not typically close sales. A classic example of such a sales job is the pharmaceutical industry detailer who visits and tries to persuade doctors to prescribe a firm's products.

Trade salespeople. Consumer packaged goods firms deploy sales reps to help customers, especially retail stores, promote their products, restock shelves, set up displays, and so forth. Trade salespeople might on occasion be asked to be order takers as well.

Technical salespeople. Firms that sell technology-intensive products employ salespeople to provide technical assistance to existing customers. These sales support personnel are usually trained engineers whose primary task is to help the field sales force manage customer relationships.

Elements of the Personal Selling Process

Although no two salespersons approach the task of selling in precisely the same way, sales is generally a multistage process that includes some or all of the following steps.

Prospecting

Prospecting—that is, generating qualified leads or finding new opportunities among the existing customer base—is the first step in the sales process. Depending on the type of business, prospecting can take many forms, including networking, seminars, marketing, trade shows, and cold calling. The purpose of this step is to identify a qualified decision maker or an ally in the organization who can help the sales rep reach the decision maker.

Evaluating and Preapproach

The next step generally is to size up the customer revenue potential and cost to pursue the opportunity. Sales reps thus need to be facile at discerning customers' true needs at a considerable level of detail. They must also determine whether prospects have the ability and authority to buy.

It is also important to set objectives for the sales effort. The objective of a sales call is not always to make a sale. For example, other objectives of sales calls include persuading prospects to agree to a product demonstration or to use a product on a trial basis. Objectives should in all cases be specific, measurable, and realistic, and have a time element.

Approaching the Customer or Making the Presentation

The old saying that first impressions are lasting and therefore important is true in selling. The key element in approaching a customer is the presentation, of which there are several types.

One approach, to provide stimuli that will initiate a purchase decision on the part of the customer, is classically exemplified by the "would you like fries with your burger?" question. Another approach, the canned presentation, is typically a memorized, repetitive spiel to which all customers interested in a specific product are treated. This approach works for products that are well known or heavily advertised. Other sales presentations are customized to the particular needs of individual customers (personal selling vs. traditional mass-media advertising). Sales reps who employ this approach ask questions first and make their presentations accordingly.

Overcoming Objections

Anticipating and countering customer objections proactively and reactively is another necessary and very important step in the sales process. Price is most commonly objected to by customers. Other types of objections include issues with the product (e.g., "I don't like the way it works," "this is not what I need"), the firm (e.g., "I don't like your firm"), timing (e.g., "I don't think now is the right time to buy"), lack of information (e.g., "I need more details before I can decide"), and competition (e.g., "I would like to check other options out before making any decision"). Overcoming objections is, in effect, also a value-building exercise in which the sales rep is called upon to provide reasons that adequately overcome customer resistance and justify the customer's purchase.

Handling objections requires very special skills. Sales reps need first to carefully listen to what their customers are saying and to what those customers' objections are. Sales reps then need to acknowledge receipt of the message, communicate their understanding of the concern, respond in a manner that overcomes the objection, and confirm that the concerns have been adequately addressed.

Closing

Closing, or testing the willingness of the prospect to buy, is the step that leads to revenue generation. Good sales reps continually test their prospects' readiness to buy using trial closings. Examples of trial closings include: How does this sound to you so far? Is there anything else you would like to know at this point? How does this compare to what you have seen for competing products? Does that answer your concern?

A series of trial closings on the heels of succesfully handling objections brings a sales rep to the actual close. Questions used to close the sale are typically direct and straightforward: Is it a deal then? When should I come to install the product? What if I could successfully resolve this problem; would you be willing to commit then?

Following Up

Following up on sales involves such activities as determining whether an order was delivered on time and installed properly and as promised. Good sales reps, simultaneously with following up to ensure that everything is going smoothly, begin prospecting the customer again to see, for example, if there is an ongoing need that can be serviced with a simple reorder or if needs have changed, revealing an opportunity to up-sell or cross-sell a new product or service.

Sales Management

The importance of managing the activities of sales reps for maximum effectiveness has already been noted. The sales management function involves the following activities.

Setting Strategic Goals and Individual Objectives

The objectives of individual salespeople should be aligned with the strategic marketing goals of the firm. Before attempting to set individual salespeople's objectives, sales management must answer questions such as: Should the firm be pursuing opportunities with new customers or deepening relationships with its existing customers? Does a new product deserve special attention because it will play a strategic role in the firm's product portfolio in the future? How should the firm position its products against the products of competing firms?

Setting its salespeople's objectives and associated sales tasks defines and communicates the role the firm expects individuals to play in the pursuit of its strategic goals. Sales management must determine how much authority to delegate to individual salespeople. For example, should management determine the number of new customers with which salespeople should meet, or should the salespeople decide whether to spend their time developing their existing base or meeting with new customers? Should management set sales targets for each of the firm's product lines or let the salespeople determine which of its products best meet their customers' needs?

More specific objectives need to be established when the goals of individual salespeople diverge from the goals of the firm, and when salespeople do not have the capacity, perhaps because they are relatively new to selling, to make good decisions on their own.

Organizing the Sales Force

How a firm organizes its sales force will depend on how it wants to interact with customers. Marketing is sometimes described as getting the right product in front of the right customer at the right time and at the right price. Whether or not this will happen depends on whether the sales force is organized in an efficient manner.

As with other channel decisions, sales force organization depends on balancing the competing concerns of control, coverage, and cost.

Control. Firms have more control over how they interact with their customers when they establish direct sales forces. This format enables management decisions to be quickly communicated to salespeople and sales managers to directly influence how the salespeople interact with customers. In contrast, firms are legally bound to keep relationships with manufacturer's representatives and sales agents at arm's length.

Coverage. Two aspects of coverage warrant attention. First, a firm needs to determine whether it wants to spend time building relationships with the customers it desires or to engage an external agent who has established relationships with these customers. Manufacturers' representatives often have such established relationships but typically have less loyalty to the manufacturer than to their customers.

Second, a firm needs to determine whether a customer's needs can be met by a single person or whether multiple people (salespeople, outside agents, or a mix of the two) are needed to serve the customer. Conflict is bound to arise when multiple people are needed. Establishing highly specific guidelines for customer interaction is easier when products and services are clearly differentiated, but problems are nonetheless inevitable when multiple people are serving a given customer.

Cost. The cost of serving customers is also a determinant of sales force organization. More coverage and more control come at increasing cost. A firm's profitability depends on adequately balancing these concerns, but decisions about how to organize a sales force are often contentious and rarely made on the basis of cost alone.

Issues to consider when organizing a sales force include the following:

- Do all customers have the same needs and use the same buying processes?

- Do our products and services require special or technical knowledge? Will we need to tightly control how we sell to customers?

- How many people will be needed to adequately cover the market?

- Should all geographies be treated the same, or are some better reached through manufacturer's representatives and others through a direct sales force?

- Is it in the manufacturer's representative's interest to work with us?

Managing Salespeople

The relationship between a firm and its salespeople begins when the firm recruits new salespeople and progresses through several stages. The firm familiarizes these individuals with its procedures and systems and might, depending on a given individual's level of experience, provide some general training in how to sell. Finally, the firm determines how to motivate, evaluate, and compensate its salespeople on an ongoing basis.

Recruiting Salespeople

Filling sales positions with the wrong people not only hurts a firm's productivity in the short run but also results in higher turnover and training costs in the long run. Recruiting the right salespeople is thus essential to building a productive sales organization; the best salespeople tend to be productive year after year, enabling a firm to achieve consistent growth.

Whether a candidate is right for a sales organization depends both on individual personality traits and on the fit between the individual's skills and the tasks that are expected to be performed. Larger firms often screen job applicants for selling aptitude by testing for personality traits such as likability, persistence, and ability to empathize. Salespeople hear no from customers much more frequently than they hear yes, and it takes special people to persist in the face of doors that are continuously closed in their faces.

Firms also need to assess the fit between an individual's skills and the job requirements. Individuals who thrive in hit-and-run transaction sales environments might not have the ability to think more strategically and succeed in selling environments that call for a lengthier, consultative approach.

Training

Various levels of training are provided to salespeople. More training is required when a consistent corporate image is an objective, when the products and services being offered are complex, when the sales cycle is long and involved, and when incoming employees have little experience in sales.

It often takes months for a salesperson to get up to speed on a firm's policies and procedures and become productive in the field. Effective training can speed this process along but cannot entirely eliminate the learning curve. Existing salespeople might be taken out of the field to be acquainted with the features and benefits of new products or how organizations in a given industry buy products, or simply to be given an opportunity to brush up on personal selling techniques.

The overarching goal of sales training is to help salespeople better explain how their firms' products and services satisfy customers' needs. In simple selling environments, this might amount to describing a product's features and closing the sale. In more complex environments, a salesperson might need to develop a deep understanding of how a customer's business works and how the company's products and services address that customer's business needs.

Supervision

In many occupations, close supervision has been shown to have a negative impact on the job satisfaction of workers who view it as reduced autonomy. Such workers might feel that the firm is "breathing down their necks." Research has shown that workers in unstructured and nonroutine jobs are happier when their superiors monitor them closely and help provide structure to their work.

Salespeople work away from the office on their customers' schedules. When prospecting new customers, they face rejection much more frequently than they enjoy success. They can spend months trying to win an account only to have a competitor come in at the last minute and take the business away from them. Customers hold them responsible for things they cannot control. Because salespeople so often face nonroutine situations and customer demands, they are more likely to desire closer supervision and direction and support to meet the demands of their jobs.

Evaluation of the Selling Effort

Although production measured against sales quota is the most common measure of sales performance, salespeople are evaluated in other ways as well. Managers critique their salespeople's strategic plans for territory development, observe their salespeople during customer visits, and use surveys to measure customer satisfaction.

The underlying goal of evaluation is to provide feedback that will help salespeople improve their future performance. Managers assess how their salespeople work with customers and suggest ways to improve those salespeople's effectiveness. They might suggest ways for their salespeople to meet new customers or improve the odds of closing business. Productivity is not the sole metric that determines whether an individual advances to higher sales positions.

Compensation

Sales compensation plans are used to motivate greater effort from salespeople and reward individuals who meet or exceed their objectives. Compensation is typically given in some combination of salary and incentives. Salary provides security to the salesperson; incentives motivate the salesperson to work harder. Financial incentives can be either behavior- or outcome-based depending on the firm's goals.

Behavior-based compensation systems reward salespeople for completing tasks regardless of whether the outcomes are positive (e.g., bonuses for calling on new customers whether or not they buy the product). Firms that employ such systems reduce risk to employees but might suffer from free-riding. Moreover, salespeople have less authority to do what is right for the customer under this type of system.

Outcome-based incentive systems reward salespeople only for positive results. This aligns the goals of the salespeople with the goals of the firm but subjects the salespeople to more risk. This sort of system can be particularly frustrating when salespeople have less control over the outcomes of their efforts or suffer a string of bad luck.

Firms also use both intrinsic and extrinsic reward systems to keep motivation high. Because salespeople tend to be goal oriented, sales quotas are commonly used as motivational tools. Companies view this tool in different ways. Sometimes, quotas are set high so that salespeople have to stretch to attain them. This strategy can work as long as the salespeople believe that the quota is attainable, but it can be damaging if the quota is viewed as utterly unrealistic. Also, salespeople having a bad year might be inclined to coast. Setting quotas at low levels in order to build confidence necessitates careful monitoring if salespeople's earnings are tied to their quotas.

Nonmonetary compensation (e.g., sporty leased cars or exotic trips) can be an effective motivational tool, especially when many salespeople are competing for the same reward. These sorts of programs often take the form of a contest in order to not only reward salespeople for a job well done but also provide public recognition of their work.

Summary

This chapter looks at how the personal selling approach to implementing a firm's marketing strategy factors into the firm's success. To increase sales performance, these firms must carefully manage their salespeople (personal selling) and sales organizations (sales management), including recruiting, training, evaluating, and compensating individuals in the unique role of being a salesperson or sales representative.

Additional Readings on Selling and Sales Management

Arnold, David J., Julian M. Birkinshaw, and Omar Toulan. "Can Selling Be Globalized? The Pitfalls of Global Account Management." *California Management Review*, October 1, 2001. Drawing on field and survey research among global account managers, this article suggests managerial guidelines for a strategic approach for effective implementation of global account management programs.

Liautaud, Bernard. "The Littlest Sales Force." *Harvard Business Review*, October 2004. The chief executive officer of a software company explains how he managed the growth of his company by building his global sales force incrementally.

Waaser, Ernest, et al. "How You Slice It: Smarter Segmentation for Your Sales Force." *Harvard Business Review*, March 2004. This article describes how the CEO of a seventy-year-old company, a top producer of hospital beds and specialty mattresses, restructured its sales organization so it could tailor its approach to its two key segments, thereby lowering the cost of sales and increasing sales and profit margins as well as customer satisfaction.

Notes

1. Summary, Additional Readings, and Notes were added to this chapter. They did not appear in the Class Note.

2. Two classic works of literature on the lives of, and interactions between, sales representatives can be found in A. Miller's play *Death of a Salesman: Certain Private Conversations in Two Acts and a Requiem* (New York: Penguin Twentieth-Century Classics, 1998), and in D. Mamet's play *Glengarry Glen Ross* (New York: Grove Press, 1992). Both are available in audio and video formats. It should be noted that a perennial best-selling trade book that has been popular among salespeople is D. Carnegie, *How to Win Friends & Influence People* (New York: Pocket, 1990). A more recent publication is J. Gitomer's *The Little Red Book of Selling: 12.5 Principles of Sales Greatness* (New York: Bard Press, 2004).

Managing Customers

A S DEFINED IN THE CHAPTER ON MARKETING strategy, marketing is the process whereby an enterprise creates value by meeting the needs of its targeted customers.[1] A firm is thus defined not only by the products it sells but also by the customers it serves. This chapter on managing customers deals with serving customers and specifically addresses the following topics:

- The importance and benefits of managing customer relationships

- Attracting and retaining the right customers

- Managing customers to maximize customer lifetime value

- Deselecting customers in a way that avoids detracting from the brand

- Respecting customers' privacy

This chapter was written by Gail McGovern and Das Narayandas and originally published as "Note on Managing Customers" Class Note 2-506-047 (Boston: Harvard Business School Publishing, 2005). It was lightly edited for consistency.

What Is Customer Relationship Management?

Customer relationship management (CRM) is an enterprise approach to understanding and influencing customer acquisition and retention. CRM is the strategic process of shaping the interactions between customers and the company in order to maximize both customer lifetime value for the firm and satisfaction for the customer. Companies that successfully design and execute systems that facilitate these interactions can enjoy a sustainable competitive advantage.

The degree to which companies establish customer relationships varies by factors such as choice of channels, industry, the competitive landscape, and the type and size of the customer base. Examples can be found in which firms with several million customers rely on face-to-face interactions; there are also instances in which companies serving a small number of customers deepen relationships through electronic commerce (see figure 9-1).

Despite the fact that customers are at the heart of any enterprise, not all firms manage individual customers. Without such an emphasis, firms will find it difficult to retain and acquire customers as those firms' existing relationships change or their customer base shifts.

FIGURE 9-1

Types of customer relationships

	Small customer base	Large customer base
Multichannel	Boeing Integrated Defense System (face-to-face, Web, phone)	Fidelity Investments (face-to-face, Web, phone)
Single-channel	Fabtek (face-to-face)	Amazon (Web-based) eBay (Web-based) Starbucks (face-to-face via baristas)

Why Is Customer Management Important?

Customer management systems are designed to enhance customer loyalty, and loyal customers generate more profits than dissatisfied or merely satisfied ones. Loyal customers tend to demonstrate a willingness to both repurchase and pay a price premium. They resist competitors' blandishments and adverse expert opinions and will generate positive word of mouth. Therefore, they generate more revenue; since they require less persuasion on an ongoing basis, they are less costly to serve as well.

Customers' needs and the value they perceive in vendors' offerings are subject to change over time. For example, products in the early stages of their life cycle are often viewed as novel, and early customers tend to be less price sensitive. But as a product matures and becomes more of a commodity, new customers enter that are more interested in service, relationships, and price. Unless the firm evolves its customer management strategy, misalignment between its offers and customers' expectations and needs will amplify, resulting in customer dissatisfaction, possible defection, and reduced prices and profitability for the company.

An increased emphasis on a set of customers within the portfolio can affect a firm's relationship with other customers currently served. Black & Decker achieved phenomenal growth in sales and profits in the 1980s as it expanded its relationship with the do-it-yourself customer base. Acquisition of the GE Spacemaker product line enabled it to offer these customers home appliances as well as power tools. But, as the firm moved from the garage into the home, its traditional tradespeople segment had difficulty identifying with the Black & Decker brand. As such, the firm had to reformulate its approach to its original customer base. Similarly, Starbucks saw a new, younger, time-pressed set of customers begin to flood its retail establishments thereby negatively impacting the experiences of the firm's loyal, established customer base. This forced Starbucks to invest in adding employees in its retail stores. CRM can facilitate these changes in relationships within the firm's portfolio.

Technological and environmental changes have occurred to the extent that firms that lack a customer management strategy will be at a competitive disadvantage. Twenty years ago, by purchasing spots on three U.S. television networks, advertisers could reach 80 percent of the population; today it would take a cost-prohibitive 150 networks. The majority of homes in the United States now have broadband access and are spending increasing amounts of their household budgets on forms of entertainment that have limited mass-media advertising. New, faster ways of communicating have emerged, and firms must provide meaningful experiences and deepening relationships with an ever more powerful consumer base. The recent explosion in inexpensive and rich customer information and customer interaction systems has enabled marketers to shift from a transactional approach that emphasizes individual exchanges to the management of customer relationships over time. Firms can now leverage customer-level information to develop strategies to manage relationships and individual interactions with each and every one of their customers.

What Value Does CRM Provide to a Firm?

Generally speaking, the most obvious benefits of CRM are in the area of segmentation. Traditional segmentation methodology (e.g., demographics, size of customer, etc.) can be enhanced with the data resident in third-party databases, which can provide clues with respect to variables such as hidden high net worth. Consequently, segmentation cells can become smaller and more precise.

This ability to microsegment provides the firm with a number of marketing advantages that can be transformational in terms of efficiency and effectiveness. These advantages can enable firms to:

- Measure, manage, and optimize the cost to serve individual customers: Companies can track revenues, channel usage, and other variable costs down to the individual customer level.

- Determine which customers are unprofitable and take remedial action: For example, unprofitable customers can be educated in the use of lower-cost, electronic channels.

- Conduct small ongoing marketing experiments with small cells of customers: This allows firms to optimize the results of future marketing campaigns.

- Measure the return on investment from marketing expenditures: Companies can compare the results of an experimental campaign performed on a small cell of customers to a control group. They can thus calculate the financial impact of a broader campaign.

- Avoid expensive, wasteful mass marketing campaigns that may not resonate with a broad set of customers: CRM facilitates smaller, more targeted programs.

- Increase revenues through customer acquisition: Companies can be more successful at putting the right offer in front of the right customer at the right time.

In addition, because a typical CRM system is dynamically updated, it becomes even more refined over time. CRM systems "learn," becoming more intelligent and self-correcting as more information is collected from marketing experiments, rep input, and so forth.

The Customer Management Process

Firms need to have a clear-cut, well-defined approach to managing their customer relationships. Typically, the customer management process entails:

- Selecting the portfolio of customers to serve ("whom do we serve?")

- Developing a corresponding portfolio of customer management strategies ("how should we serve them?")

- Monitoring the health of customer relationships over time ("are they happy with us?")

- Linking their customer management effort to economic reward—that is, customer profitability ("are we making money?")

How well a firm monitors the health of customer relationships will determine the degree to which it is able to quantify the costs and benefits associated with customer relationship, which, in turn, will influence its decision about which customers to continue to serve.

Selecting Customers

Marketing strategy has always emphasized the importance of market selection. With a lot at stake, including enormous investments of resources, firms spend significant amounts of time in defining the businesses they are in. Customer selection requires the same discipline since every customer can have a significant impact on a firm's profits.

The familiar phrase "known by the company one keeps" is very apropos to customers. Firms need to be mindful that their choice of customers will define their skill set over time ("whom we serve affects who we are"), and, in turn, their abilities affect their choice of customers ("who we are affects whom we can serve").

For example, through a rash of opportunistic customer selection decisions, Fabtek, a small industrial titanium fabricator, landed in an anomalous situation of operating unprofitably at full capacity with dissatisfied customers who were complaining about project delays. Fabtek's capacity and capabilities affected the orders it could satisfactorily serve, highlighting the point that "who we are affects whom we can serve," and the fact that each order was likely to pull Fabtek in a different direction calls to mind the dictum "whom we serve affects who we are." As this case illustrates, companies should acquire customers that they can best serve and that in turn deliver value over their lifetime.

Developing Customer Management Strategies to Maximize Customer Profitability

The process of designing appropriate customer management strategies should enhance customer value and maximize customer profitability. There are different approaches to maximizing customer profitability. By definition, profits are the difference between customer response (sales revenues) and the firm's costs to serve the customer. Profits can therefore be increased either by increasing revenues or decreasing selling effort.

While firms' approaches to maximizing customer profitability can be different, they are similar in the way they monitor the health of their customer relationships using a combination of actual customer behaviors (e.g., revenues generated) and leading indicators that measure customer attitudes and intent (e.g., satisfaction surveys). By having a finger on the pulse of the relationship, firms can make appropriate changes in the way they manage customer relationships and maximize long-term customer profitability.

Choices among investment opportunities typically rely on evaluations of anticipated return on investments (ROI) and associated risks. The same logic must be applied to investments in customer management strategies. To accurately calculate customer profitability and remove inefficiencies in current customer management efforts, firms need information about the impact of individual actions on the revenue generated and costs incurred in a customer relationship. Linking specific cost elements with the customer revenue stream enables firms to isolate and remove inefficiencies in the customer management effort.

The lag and cumulative effect between vendor effort and customer response can thwart attempts to isolate cause-effect relationships between different company actions and corresponding customer reactions. The best option under these circumstances is to calculate an overall ROI for a customer over time using a lifetime value approach.

In general, **lifetime value (LTV)** for a customer is calculated as shown in figure 9-2.

When margin is relatively fixed across periods, one can simplify that expression by assuming an infinite economic life (i.e., letting $N \to \infty$) which leads to:

$$LTV = \frac{M}{1 - r + i} - AC$$

Although the sophistication of LTV models makes them excellent tools for valuing customers, the value of the models reflects the accuracy of the data inputs. Firms should therefore make every effort to drive revenue and cost causation down to the individual customer level.

FIGURE 9-2

Lifetime value equation

$$LTV = \sum_{a=1}^{N} \frac{(M_a)r^{(a-1)}}{(1 + i)^a} - AC$$

where:
N = the number of years over which the relationship is calculated
M_a = the margin the customer generates in year a
r = the retention rate ($r^{(a-1)}$ is the survival rate for year a).
i = the interest rate
AC = the acquisition cost

Deselecting Unprofitable Customers

Once the tools are in place to measure individual customer profitability, companies often become aware of entire segments of unprofitable customers. When a firm considers "firing" unprofitable customers, they must tread lightly. When a company actively elects to terminate its relationships with a segment of customers, there may be far-reaching impact on the firm's brand. The seemingly low-value customer could turn out to be the nephew of the firm's most valued client! Thus, companies should consider the customer, public relations, and brand impacts of their actions.

Respecting Customer Privacy

Customer relationship management provides firms with a powerful tool to understand their customers in ways that were previously impossible. With third-party databases, firms can purchase information regarding credit history, income, assets, demographics, and so forth. By entrusting reps with this sort of data, companies are in effect expecting their reps to understand precisely where to draw the line between personalization and privacy. Therefore, a clear, transparent privacy policy should be established for both the reps' use and customers' edification.

Common Customer Management Pitfalls

Many firms that adopt CRM processes are under the false impression that the biggest single challenge has to do with technology implementation (i.e., developing the set of marketing tools and software, etc.). However, technology is only a small piece of the overall puzzle.

Rather, the more fundamental problem is that companies often embark on CRM projects with lofty but imprecise goals, or they develop goals at the tactical level without an appreciation for what CRM adoption implies for the overall strategic philosophy of the firm. This lack of strategy and precision ultimately causes confusion as to whether the CRM system is adding to or subtracting from the bottom line. (See figure 9-3.)

Furthermore, many firms overestimate the IT complexities of CRM but woefully underestimate the human complexity associated with a shift in strategic philosophy. Recalcitrant sales personnel or service reps can bring the system to its failure point, especially when these reps fail to recognize the personal benefits of entering and maintaining customer data. Similarly, the firm's marketing organization may lack the skills to make the strategic leap from mass marketing to direct marketing, and may balk at the notion of financial accountability.

At Fidelity, managers made a huge investment in CRM, spending $75 million in IT, financial systems, campaign management, and rep training to implement the system. Surprisingly, the IT project, which was a remarkably complex systems integration challenge, turned out to be relatively easy. The nonhuman aspects of CRM—personalizing the Web, direct mail, and e-mail commu-

FIGURE 9-3

Customer relationship management process

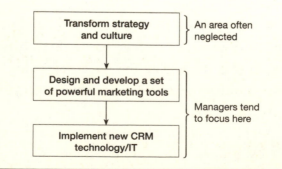

nications—also turned out to be relatively easy. These elements were measurable and controllable; marketers could see the results of each campaign, measured against a control group.

What Fidelity did not anticipate was the huge cultural shift required to successfully implement CRM. Reps had to change the ways they interacted with customers, populate the databases, utilize the triggers, and make outbound calls. In fact, the reps needed to make a cultural shift from a strictly service-driven culture to a sales-driven mentality as well. Meanwhile, customers suddenly found themselves receiving outbound calls from Fidelity and having proactive conversations with reps. In addition, marketers were being measured and held accountable for the first time. Finally, Fidelity needed to make decisions involving privacy, third-party databases, and resegmentation. In short, the skills that were required were outside of the organization's historical comfort zone.

An important related learning is that successful execution of these CRM tactics can only be achieved if the correct internal metrics are in place; without these metrics, employees will lack the incentive to make the necessary behavior changes upon which the CRM system relies.

Steps to Facilitate Success

Companies that embark on CRM implementations would be well served to take proactive steps to avoid the pitfalls mentioned in this chapter. They should:

- Set clear, measurable ROI targets (simply having a goal of "increasing customer satisfaction," e.g., is not enough)

- Align employee compensation with the results of these initiatives

- Obtain buy-in across the organization every step of the way (by including sales and service reps in the development process, firms will, by default, be creating "missionaries" to help drive adoption)

- Drive the initiative from the senior-most levels in the firm

- Ensure that employees' skills are compatible with the demands created by CRM

- Align strategy, tactics, and measurements throughout every level of the organization

Summary

This chapter looks at how companies go about serving customers, specifically establishing and managing customer relationships, recruiting and retaining the right (i.e., profitable) customers, managing those customers to maximize their lifetime value to the company, letting unprofitable customers go without detracting from the brand, and respecting and securing customers' privacy from third parties, especially those intent on using customer information deleteriously or illegally.

Additional Readings on Customer Management[2]

Dowling, Grahame R. "Customer Relationship Management: In B2C Markets, Often Less Is More." *California Management Review*, April 1, 2002. This article critically examines the assumptions that underpin CRM and suggests that companies should adopt CRM only after carefully appraising its cost effectiveness.

Gulati, Ranjay, and James B. Oldroyd. "The Quest for Customer Focus." *Harvard Business Review*, April 2005. This article explains that getting closer to customers isn't about building an information technology system; it's about forging a companywide relationship with customers, starting with a repository containing every customer interaction with the company, organized by customer and not by company unit or representative.

Rigby, Darrell K., and Dianne Ledingham. "CRM Done Right." *Harvard Business Review*, November 2004. The authors have distilled the experiences of companies that lead in the implementation of CRM practices into the four questions that all companies should ask themselves as they launch their own CRM initiatives.

Winer, Russell S. "A Framework for Customer Relationship Management." *California Management Review*, July 1, 2001. This article develops a comprehensive CRM model incorporating seven phases of successful CRM execution—namely, database creation, analysis of the database, customer selection, customer targeting, relationship marketing, privacy issues, and new metrics necessary for evaluating the CRM effort.

Notes

1. Summary, Additional Readings, and Notes were added to this chapter. They did not appear in the Class Note.

2. For in-depth analysis of customer equity, see S. Gupta and D. Lehmann, *Managing Customers as Investments: The Strategic Value of Customers in the Long Run* (Philadelphia: Wharton School Publishing, 2005), and R. C. Blattberg, G. Getz, and J. S. Thomas, *Customer Equity: Building and Managing Relationships as Valuable Assets* (Boston: Harvard Business School Press, 2001).

Index